Julian Schnabel: *Paintings 1975 - 1986*

Julian Schnabel

Paintings 1975 - 1986

WHITECHAPEL

19 September - 26 October 1986

Lenders to the exhibition

Galerie Bruno Bischofberger, Zürich
Mary Boone Gallery, New York
Arthur and Carol Goldberg, New York
Janet Green, London
Gerald Just, Hannover
Aron and Phyllis Katz, Boulder, Colorado
Mr. and Mrs. Robert Kaye, New Jersey
Lannan Foundation, Venice, California
Saatchi Collection, London
Jacqueline Schnabel, New York
Julian Schnabel, New York
Barbara and Eugene M. Schwartz, New York
Speyer Family Collection, New York
Musée National d'Art Moderne,
Centre Georges Pompidou, Paris
Private Collection

The exhibition has been organised by the Whitechapel Art Gallery in conjunction with the Centre Georges Pompidou, Paris, and will be shown at the following venues:

Whitechapel Art Gallery, London (19 September – 26 October 1986)
Musée National d'Art Moderne, Centre Georges Pompidou, Paris (14 January – 15 March 1987)
Städtische Kunsthalle Düsseldorf (29 April – 8 June 1987)

Acknowledgments

The Whitechapel Art Gallery has long had a reputation as a space in which contemporary painting and sculpture can be presented to advantage in the best natural light for consideration by artists, critics and a wider public. The Julian Schnabel exhibition extends a series of exhibitions of work by American artists shown at the Whitechapel since 1958, initiated by Bryan Robertson with memorable exhibitions such as Pollock, Rothko, Johns and Rauschenberg and continued more recently with Hesse, Shapiro, Marden and Guston. Such projects can only be realized with the close cooperation of the artist, his or her gallery representative and collectors of the work, and with the collaboration of other institutions.

In this instance we were fortunate to gain the support of the lenders mentioned elsewhere in this catalogue, Arnold and Mark Glimcher of the Pace Gallery, New York and Dominique Bozo, Alfred Pacquement, Bernard Blistène and Martine Silie of the Centre Georges Pompidou, Paris. We are indebted to them all for their endeavours on our behalf.

We are most grateful to Tom McEvilley for an essay which establishes the context for consideration of Schnabel's work and to the artist's assistants, Sylvie Ball and Mark Wilson, for their contribution to the realization of the exhibition.

Julian Schnabel has been an enthusiastic and understanding collaborator, recognising the need to make an exhibition which would cover the range of his work. We hope that the exhibition will also contain some surprises for him, in paintings that he has not seen for some time.

Contents

Julian Schnabel, 1982
Photograph by Hans Namuth

Foreword

When 'success' and attention come rapidly, as they did for Julian Schnabel during 1979, it is often difficult to remember that the very paintings which have changed our vision were born out of a mood of opposition to established ways of looking.

Schnabel, regarded by 1980/81 as one of the leading spirits in a new generation of painters, and taken up by the fashionable media, was not always so close to the centre. Many good artists remain unnoticed for longer than he did, but it is nevertheless remarkable to consider just how unfashionable were his concerns in 1975/76. It is a measure of how far the terms of critical debate have changed and, I believe, the degree to which Schnabel himself contributed to that change by the sheer force and ambition of his work.

In the early seventies the studios of many young painters of Schnabel's generation were filled with canvases which paid homage to Newman and Reinhardt and reflected the example of Ryman, Marden and Mangold. Schnabel sought other models and, although for a short period the surface quality of his paintings owed something to the use of oil and encaustic by Brice Marden, he began to look to Europe rather than to America as a grounding for his work.

This distinct shift, many years ahead of the critics and the 'market' of which he is so often regarded as being merely the product, is one of the main strengths of his art. It still distinguishes his work from that of other American artists of his generation. Early on Schnabel had been interested in the work of the German expatriate Richard Lindner but now, in approaching Europe, Schnabel took a characteristically singular course. Rather than choose the German Expressionists and the Neue Sächlichkeit artists who were at the root of Lindner's art and who were being re-assessed in a series of exhibitions through the seventies, he decided instead to follow the example of Twombly in Italy and, slightly later, of Beuys in Düsseldorf. From the standpoint of New York in the mid seventies, such choices must have seemed eccentric. Yet in Europe Schnabel had discovered an art in which allusion could play a significant role.

In the media Schnabel is regarded as a 'neo-expressionist' and his work is linked to the so-called 'wild' German painting of Penck, Lüpertz and Baselitz, but his sensibility is in fact much closer to that of Düsseldorf than to Berlin; to Polke, Broodthaers, Beuys and especially to the pupils of Beuys – Kiefer and Palermo. As in the work of these artists, meaning in Schnabel's art is layered, shifting and elusive. This 'European' sensibility is especially noticeable in Schnabel's drawings and in some of the more recent paintings on velvet and tarpaulin, which are distinguished by an ambiguity of space and subtlety of touch. It is such works which undermine the view that he is simply a maker of large bombastic paintings on grounds of broken crockery.

This exhibition is therefore planned, in part, to correct a simplistic reading of an artist who is capable of many moods and many subjects. There is a surprising lack of familiarity with the work amongst critics, collectors, museum curators and the wider public who have not chosen, or have been unable, to follow the development of Schnabel's range. Some, no doubt, have been discouraged by the media attention to Schnabel's personality, but this in itself is not new, and should not now be allowed to obscure the fact that we are evaluating an artist who has himself helped to shape the climate and terms in which we discuss the art of the eighties. That alone is rare enough to warrant consideration; the paintings themselves offer additional rewards.

Nicholas Serota

Julian Schnabel, working on *Prison: Waiting for an Ultra-Violet Ray,* 1985
Photograph by Hans Namuth

The Case of Julian Schnabel

Thomas McEvilley

The outcries of the art world in the last decade or so have floated up from deep rifts in the culture as a whole. Our sense of history, and with it of ourselves, is changing. This is a story that can be read in the art of that period, for it expressed the spirit of its age as much as the individual sensibilities of artists, even in cases where expression and sensibility seemed especially prominent. The case of Julian Schnabel is a special paradigm of this, special both in the furor that has surrounded it and in what it reveals. No one expected him. No one knew they wanted him. Yet somehow the age demanded him, and he seems to be here to stay. There is nothing anyone can do about it. The market's adulation of him and the critics' frequent hostility towards him are two ramifications of one fact: that Schnabel has been received as a champion of the resurgence of Modernism, which is dear to the market, and implicitly as a destroyer of Post-Modernism, which is dear to many critics. If, as is widely presumed, he wishes to carry on the Modernist project, then the Post-Modernist project (which is, roughly speaking, to save the human ambitions of Modernism from the insane overconfidence of its methods) is retarded. So he has been received in certain quarters as a symbol of regression. Much of the literature on him sounds like an attempt to exorcise him right out of the Post-Modern community. The devil that is being symbolically exorcised through him is Will; an aspect of human selfhood with which this artist has been especially associated in the critical consensus that has emerged around him. The controversy involves ideological differences over the two great topics of recent art: self and history. It is a late scene in a drama of great importance that has been building up now for two centuries or more.

In the nineteenth century, history was viewed as a more or less linear progression toward a goal that was loosely defined yet awesomely impressive. The philosopher Hegel formulated this goal somewhat mythically as the self-realization of universal Spirit, which was to be accomplished through history and would also constitute the end of history, through attainment of the perfect state. This process, it was believed, would not unfold entirely spontaneously. It needed human assistance, and this is why Hegel called history 'Work'. Will was the essence of getting the Work done. To put history over the top, certain human leaders of special importance ('world-historical individuals') would have to exercise Will with a focus and intensity that go far beyond the ordinary, that are, precisely, heroic. What is necessary for such an exercise is an heroic selfhood crystalline in integrity while rugged enough to enforce its designs on the world. Napoleon was the great example and Beethoven's *Heroic Symphony* the affadavit.

Responding to the socio-political macrocosm around it, the art world redefined itself in terms of heroic selfhood, the Work of history, and the Goal. A metaphysical, crypto-religious way of talking about art became common. Hegel himself, for example, said that great art was the embodiment of the absolute; it already contained in some way the goal that history in general was driving towards. That this was a contradiction in terms (if it is embodied, it is no longer the absolute) did not trouble anyone at the beginning of the Romantic era. A.W. Schlegel who, along with his brother Friedrich, first defined Romantic art, described beauty as 'a symbolical representation of the infinite'. Hegel's friend and colleague Schelling brought the contradiction back into the open, saying that art was the resolution of an infinite conflict in a finite object. More importantly, Schelling proposed a revision of priorities that would have tremendous influence. Kant had said that the aesthetic, ethical and cognitive faculties were equal and separate. Hegel agreed more or less when he said that art, religion and philosophy were three equal channels to Spirit. Schelling, however, said that the aesthetic faculty was the highest, the most innately spiritual and transcendent, and this was to be a characteristic belief of the Romantic era. Hegel had emphasized the nation state as the means of advancing Spirit. Yet the elevation of art above all other human affairs almost forced the conclusion that art, not statecraft, is the activity most suitable for attaining the goal of history. This idea was intensely appealing to artists, poets, and their admirers. It found expression in Percy Bysshe Shelley's famous claim that poets are the unacknowledged legislators of mankind. Though politics and the state might be the mainstream, the hidden avantgarde that led them onward was made up of visionary poets with their eyes fixed on the beyond. For the Fine Arts, Hegel's student Karl Schnaase formulated a parallel doctrine that remained, however hidden, a part of the foundation of Modernist art theory and of the exalted Modernist view of the artist's role. Loosely expressed, the doctrine was that the destiny of art is nothing less than to be a force that forges ahead of the rest of society and leads or drags history towards the moment when all nature will be reabsorbed into Spirit. The universal culmination, then, was

not really to be attained through the efforts of statesmen, though in terms of exoteric history it may seem so; the pathway to its attainment was first to be explored by the efforts of artists, who alone work with the highest human faculty and whose productions actually contain reflections or microcosms of the absolute. The poet by placing one word beside another, the painter by placing one colour beside another, could effect ontological changes. In the specialized cult of the arts that grew in proportion as the authority of Christianity declined, these were the new world-historical individuals. That Napoleonic Will, that would lead history to its culmination would be therefore, not military or political will conquering and unifying nations, but aesthetic will engaged in the solution of formal problems through intuitions of the Unspeakable. The truest hero would be not a soldier, or leader of masses, but an artist bold in his lonely quest for the absolute. I say 'his' because one consequence of this doctrine was the continued exclusion of women, whom our inherited tradition does not warrant as heroes, from serious consideration in the art making activity. In the Romantic ideology, if an artist is not a hero exploring the transcendent unknown, then his or her work is not engaged in the sublime quest which it is the highest destiny of art to fulfil.

It was just the moment, or century, for such a myth to take hold. Darwinism and the Industrial Revolution seemed to prove that a linear, upward directionality, an actual force of progress, was inherent in both nature and culture. A general decline in the influence of established religion over the preceding century had created a climate in which spiritual intensity was available to be channelled into other activities. The religio-spiritual approach to poetry and the arts, as Matthew Arnold noted, buffered the shock of de-Christianization. The development of industrial states left in its wake countless alienated individuals for whom such a private way to be more important than the leaders of those states, at least in one's own mind (like Goethe's Werther transcendently enchanted by the literary hoax of the Ossian poems) offered the most intense gratification.

In painting, the mid nineteenth century realisms fostered an inspiring addendum, one which is also basic to the myth of Western art history. According to this myth, articulated by Roger Fry and others, art since the Stone Age has striven for the objective representation of nature. This was its first great project. Around the time of Giotto this quest became increasingly focused and remained so for four hundred years. A major milestone was the development of perspectival rendering in the Renaissance (somewhat aggressively ignoring the evidence that it had already been used by Greek and Roman painters, lost in the Middle Ages and regained from rediscovered classical sources in the Florence of Alberti and Brunelleschi). With that event, the myth goes, the objective rendering of the external world first became possible; over the following centuries modes of representation worked steadily towards complete objectivity, which was attained at last with the mid nineteenth century realisms and early Impressionism. At that moment art, having mastered the representation of nature, was driven, by the inner directive of its historical destiny, to transcend it. Having mastered nature art must enter Spirit directly. The stage, in other words, was set for abstract art, which would extend the mastery of representation from physical nature to the sublime and the absolute. This was the grand and sacred vocation of abstract art, nothing less than the attainment of pure Spirit and the culmination of history. It was this that lent such fervour to formalist pronouncements, and such breathless excitement to the work of artists who, like Jackson Pollock, for example, were regarded as 'world-historical', as altering by their work the whole history of the world.

Of course, a heavy dose of Christian millennialism was hidden in this myth; the restoration of Eden can be sensed in the end of history, the second coming of the Messiah in the role of the hero, and so on. In the continuing decline of Christian authority and the increasing alienation of the individual from the ever larger, technological state, this doctrine exercised a powerful sway. A central current of twentieth century art developed under its spell. Kasimir Malevich and Wassily Kandinsky believed all or most of it at some level of their personalities, as did Piet Mondrian, Lucio Fontana, Yves Klein, Barnett Newman, Mark Rothko, Jackson Pollock and countless other Modernists of transcendental inclination. Formalist criticism, which always involved a religious kind of feeling, assumed it for the most part, though sometimes remained unspoken. The myth strode among us like a veritable god, a god built, of course, in our image and answering to our sense of self-importance. It said that we were free to bring history to heel before our dream of Eden. By mid-century its enchantment was so intense that artists such as Yves Klein and Ad Reinhardt could believe that they were making the last, or next to last, artworks, the works that would herald and precede the final absorption of nature into Spirit. The incredible psychological pressure of this Messianic/prophetic role is one of the sources of the extremity of anxiety that characterizes so much twentieth century art and the lives of so many artists committed to the Work, and is the principal source of our obsession with the artist's person.

This delusion was deeply out of touch with other important currents of twentieth century thought, like a holy relic lying in an automobile showroom. Since the eighteenth century there had been another aspect of Modernism, not transcendentalist but sceptical, positivistic, and critical in thrust, which had been undermining mythic claims about the self and history. From David Hume to Jacques Lacan the self fell prey to various dissections and analyses. Marx broke it down into by-products of impersonal socio-economic conditions. For Darwin it was the result of biological forces. Freud saw it as a bag of disconnected and warring energies, none with much personality. For behaviourists it was a machine to be programmed. Structuralism and Post-Structuralism saw it as a more or less random group of superimposed codes. Yet still, in the theology of formalist Modernism, the myth of the world-historical individual survived, and so great was the spell of the heroic myth that much of the ambient culture, encountering it for the most part only in movies like *Lust for Life,* was grudgingly impressed and let it be.

The influence of this myth peaked in the fifties, when the imminence of pure Spirit seemed palpable in the charged air of Abstract-Expressionism. The crises of the sixties forced a revision. As so many attempted to be 'world-historical', to lay their hands directly on history and bend it to their will, but failed, the myth lost credibility. What is called the transition to Post-Modernism occurred at the moment when significant numbers of people realized with surprise that they no longer could believe in the inherent force of progress, the exalted mission of history, and the inevitability of its accomplishment. Those critical forces that had already been present came to the fore, and were now called Post-Modernism.

From the point of view called Post-Modern, every major element of the Modernist myth was reversed. The belief in progress came to seem a dangerous superstition that had led, through blind faith in the value of technological advance, to a century of global wars and the development of endgame weaponry that was truly sublime in Edmund Burke's sense of dark, vast, terrifying, infinite, and annihilating. The idea that evolution involves a direction and that history has a particular shape inherent in it came to look like wish-projections. The idea that art is the primary means of access to spiritual advancement came to feel like a mystification that served a variety of purposes, not only buffering the shock of de-Christianization but also, more sinisterly, eliminating art as a force for social change. Seen in this way Post Modernism is an attempted corrective to the myth of Modernism, which by its apotheosis of human Will had led practically to the ruin of the world and the discrediting of the whole project of civilization.

What we have not seen so clearly is that the term Post-Modern itself involves an element of wishful thinking. It implies a new age, whereas history suggests that what we are calling Post-Modernism is probably only an oscillation in a process that has been going on in the West since the faith-reason controversy in the twelfth century. This process, which underlies much of the peculiar dynamic of Western culture, is a constant wrestling between the Judeo-Christian and Greco-Roman limbs of our heritage, one of which always has the upper hand. These are the forces reflected, respectively, in the conflicting transcendentalist and critical urges of our culture. What we have called Post-Modernism may be only a temporary ascendancy of the critical over the transcendentalist mood. There is no telling how long this end of the oscillation will last, but it may not be very long.

Around 1980 signs of a resurgence of Modernism became so prominent that they could not be ignored. In the art world this resurgence centred around so-called Neo-Expressionist painting, which was received as the polar opposite of Post-Modern appropriational art, and around Schnabel in particular. The extraordinary intensity of feeling about him as an individual, or rather about this conspicuous career success, derives from an exaggerated sense that his celebrity actually endangers history, or anyway that it is an expression of a real danger to history, by reestablishing the notions of Will and artistic heroism that we so recently escaped from. This feeling is encapsulated in the common journalistic comparison of Schnabel with Pollock, an artist who, along with Picasso, Schnabel has acknowledged as an important influence on his work. Most of the journalistic treatment of this claimed relationship has focused not on the artwork (one gets the feeling often that the critic was too angry to really look at or think about the artwork) but on the person of the artist. It is implied that Schnabel is falsely pretending to the 'world-historical' role of Pollock as a mere marketing posture. In the work itself, certain similarities between Pollock's paintings and Schnabel's are obvious, especially the activation of the whole picture surface in Pollock's drip paintings of 1947-1950 and in Schnabel's plate paintings; the dimly implied figuration of Pollock's work before and after that period, and of much of Schnabel's oeuvre, and so on. Still, the emphasis on this comparison with Pollock is inherently polemical, having as much to do with ethical as with formal matters. For the fact is that Schnabel's abstractions relate to a large body of Modernist painting by many artists, some who have been influences on

him, including Cy Twombly and Joseph Beuys, and others who have not, including Robert Motherwell, a comparison too often made, William Baziotes, whose work Schnabel barely knows, and many others. In any case, the critical use of the connection with Pollock has focused not on precisely art historical elements but on the idea, repugnant to a Post-Modern attitude, of the artist as Romantic visionary hero.

Pollock's reputation of course has held up extremely well recently as Rothko's has seemed to decline somewhat and certain others of the New York School have almost dropped out of the discourse for the moment. Pollock's presence in our art consciousness thirty years after his death is very revealing, especially since everything that he supposedly stood for has supposedly been superceded. Our memory of Pollock is like a dim but reverberating memory of a god or monster who strode among us; we discuss him like the people of Geatland talking about Beowulf or Grendel – either one. A startling array of artists today (not to mention the critics, who cannot stop talking about him) point to Pollock as an inspiration for their work, or use him as an icon of one kind or another, and not only in America. In Europe Jannis Kounellis speaks about the epic wholeness of the picture space in Pollock's paintings, which, for Kounellis, pointed beyond the painting to the three-dimensional installation. Art and Language used Pollock's style in appropriational works that comment on East-West ideological differences. In New York, Mike Bidlo associated himself through performance with the Pollock myth, recreating famous incidents from his life as well as making facsimile copies of his works. There is an interesting relationship between the Pollockisms of these two young artists, Schnabel and Bidlo, who were both born about the time of Pollock's death. Bidlo openly acted out the Pollock myth and copied his works, surrounding these acts with a sense of Post-Modern irony. Schnabel denied acting out the myth, did not openly copy the work, yet has had the myth attached to him in a heavy-handed manner lacking irony and distance. In a sense Schnabel was more direct or naive than others in his mode of relating to Pollock. He attempted to take painting a step farther than Pollock, while not losing the qualities that Pollock had inscribed in the medium. The insistence on an art historical obligation to maintain continuity through sequences of formal developments is of course fundamentally Modernist; Post-Modernist art has apotheosized contrary qualities, such as discontinuity and lack of formal progression.

Many writers on Schnabel have seemed outraged by his attempt to string out the formal series that Pollock was involved in even further. Some feel that the serious attempt to advance Pollock's project as a living artistic lineage betrays Post-Modern insights into the relationship between history and human will. The ambition is helplessly permeated by the heroic personality dimension that has been attached, irrevocably it seems, to Pollock after his death. The myth of Pollock, of course, presumes that he made a direct or authentic cultural or creative statement, a statement existentially pure and arising only from world-historical intuitions. That Schnabel should attempt such a statement today, a statement not mediated, like Kounellis's, by a new medium or, like Bidlo's, by irony and implied scepticism, is taken as a naive assertion of wholeness of selfhood, a pretentious claim to an archaic type of heroic integrity, both regressive and hybristic. Today, to practise *tachisme* without irony seems an ideological statement.

Some of this criticism has been confusedly Modernist itself, expressing the feeling that Pollock was the real hero whom it is pretentious for anyone now to emulate. Heroism, in this view, was real in the Modernist period, but is now unreal. Other critics, in a more Post-Modern mood, have seen Schnabel's Pollockism not as an ersatz attempt to regain the heroism that Pollock really had, so much as a calculated attempt to revive the myth of heroism that was as wrong in Pollock's day as it is now. Schnabel's feeling that his work somehow continues the project that Pollock was involved with can seem abominable to either the Modernist or the Post-Modernist critic. Yet if Pollock's art was real, and there is surprisingly little scepticism on that point from any quarter at all, then the linking of later stylistic developments to it is merely art historical business as usual.

In the brief age of the ascendancy of conceptual art, of course, the death of painting was widely proclaimed. Painting brought with it the whole ethical burden of Modernism and its failure. To paint was to be regressive. Yet painting did not go away. Our culture showed a profound and intense need for it, perhaps in part because the problematics of our culture had articulated themselves visually through painting for at least five centuries and it is therefore in painting that they can be immediately confronted. Still, the function of painting changed. Post-Modern painting evolved types of works whose motives were very far from those of Pollock or Picasso. In America and Great Britain particularly, painting came to be practised with a conceptual deconstructive force that revealed itself in various ways, including quoting and simulation, the prominent incorporation of verbal elements and, less frequently, elements of performance very different from Action Painting as performance, and the inclusion of a variety of contents that signified social involvement and a

critical stance towards classical modernists myths such as the heroic self. But Schnabel's work, like that of certain European artists today, demonstrates something like an old-style enthusiasm for painting. His first New York show, in 1979, was perceived as instrumental in what was called, apocalyptically, like the Second Coming, 'The Return of Painting', that is, of painting that wished to continue the Modernist line instead of deconstructing it. The Post-Modern dread of, and rage at, Modernism singled him out as the new champion of the old-style self and its disasters. As Modernism resurged, he was seen as an enemy of women artists, of conceptual artists in whatever form, of critical rather than visionary art, and so on. His personal career interacted violently with the struggle between two views of history, as he was tossed about by the waves of the moment.

Prominent among those waves was the shifting of the market. Since transcendental Modernism was more saleable than deconstructive Post-Modernism, the resurgence of Modernism was seen by some as brought about not by artistic but by market forces. The market success of Schnabel and others suggested they were childishly complicit, that is, that they were being used and going along with it. Meanwhile what was taking place under the guise of their self-expression was the forced return of the feeling of isolated heroism, of heroism not dependent on the web of events but transcendently confident in its ability to make events dependent on the hero's will. The dramatic suddenness of the Neo-Expressionist flood, with Schnabel at the crest of the wave, lent it an air of heroic or Napoleonic conquest.

Yet this heroic air, many suspected, was itself faked. According to this view, the original Expressionists had indeed attained a totally direct unmediated apprehension of things, an eye that saw with the innocence of the child in romantic poetry, and so on. The Neo-Expressionists of the eighties, on the other hand, hopelessly corrupted by money and media, feigned ersatz simulations of the products of such childlike vision. To this way of thinking, Neo-Expressionism seems an ultimate betrayal of art's claim to an innocent vision, an ultimate sell-out of expression to pretence. Hidden in this view is the unconsidered assumption that a completely innocent expressiveness is a real possibility. One can sniff a trace of transcendentalist Modernism in that assumption, a misty-eyed Utopianism masking a traditional Christian yearning for Eden. To postulate an unmediated direct apprehension is to postulate a consciousness just born an instant before, not yet imprinted with prejudices, associations, and a mixed bag of motives pulling in different directions. It is a variant of the myth of the hero who grew

13

up in the forest and emerged from it a great singer because he had been talking with the birds throughout his childhood. The old romantic myth of the innocence of the artist is hidden here, of the artist's freedom from ordinary causality. But innocence, of course, is not required for expression, and may even preclude it (what could an innocent have to express?). A true innocent must not even have been exposed to the corrupting categories of language. When Kandinsky, Nolde, Kirchner and others talked of pure, instinctive, immediate expressiveness they were, of course, fooling themselves. This is not to say that they did not enter states of intense concentration, but that such states are not primally innocent and are, furthermore, still available to an artist, or to anyone else, today.

Beyond the invocation of market forces, little has been written about how Neo-Expressionism relates to its age. The answer is to be found not by looking angrily at photographs of young media-celebrated artists, but by looking analytically into their work. History expresses itself in the work, and the self reveals itself through the sense of history. In the last decade the subject of history has dominated much art, not just art history, or our own history, but the question of the whole nature of history: is it a force? a presence? a projection? a fantasy? a myth? a con game? What shape does it have (if any)? Where is it going (if anywhere)? What kind of hold does it have on us, really?

Abstract-Expressionism displayed a related concern with self and history, but in a different mood. In that case, metaphysical approaches to time, and sublimist approaches to the idea of an ultimate origin, were the characteristic products. The heroic self was presented as attaining the sublime and being dissolved in it. As history, in the Modernist view, will end by transcending itself, so will the hero. It is the end of the hero's activity to have used self to such extreme purpose as finally to transcend it by an arrival or return to the absolute source of all selfhood. Pollock's *The Deep*, Newman's *Day One*, and countless other works of the era, celebrated this idea. These approaches have since been rendered archaic by the ascendancy of a more critical, less transcendentalist attitude. Artists have been processing instead, in visual and other modes, critical, questioning, doubting or inquiring approaches to the theme of history. There is a rich range of positions available between the metaphysical version of history, which believes that it is a force with an inherent direction and meaning, and, at the other end of the spectrum, a purely critical or phenomenalistic view which holds simply that moments follow one another with no shape, direction, or meaning to the process except those which we might project onto it.

At one end of the spectrum we find artists like Kounellis, one of the great exponents of the subject of history, whose approach is primarily a classical Modernist one. He wants artistic and social commitment to the Modernist idea of progress. At the other end of the spectrum are the works of the appropriators, which openly confute the idea of the shape of history, reducing it to absurdity and attempting to neutralize or de-mystify our view of it. Schnabel's work falls in between. It is an expression of a moment when one view of history is just giving way to another. His approach is neither that of an unreconstructed Modernist nor that of a detached Post-Modernist. He represents a position that mingles elements of Modernism and Post-Modernism; a position that seems, really, that of most of our culture. Spokesmen for one position or the other tend to present them as absolutes, giving the impression that one is either a Modernist or a Post-Modernist and there is nothing in between. There is a classical Modernist puritanism to this approach which invalidates it from the start as an instrument with which to measure Post-Modernism. In fact, except for the crystalline utterances of spokesmen, the whole culture is strewn along that confused ground in between.

One of the characteristic motifs that recent art has used to portray relations between self and history is fragmentation. A whole aesthetics of the fragment has developed. This motif is central to Schnabel's oeuvre, appearing most obviously in the so-called plate paintings. In these works a wooden ground is prepared by fixing broken ceramic ware to it with Bondo. Some shards lie convexly, some concavely, some stand out at an oblique or right angle. Paint and a variety of other materials are applied over this ground. Some critics have felt that the images that appear on these grounds are less important than the grounds themselves. It is in any case true that whatever image appears in these works must lie upon that ground, and that the ground is itself a signifier through which the image must be seen and understood. The ground contains the images not only physically but in their meaning.

The first significance of the crockery ground is its brokenness. It presents an underlying condition of brokenness as the screen onto which any and all images must be projected. This brokenness, while by no means identical to Pollock's allover drip ground, is related to them. After a period when awareness of their content was repressed, the drip grounds have rightly been recognized as cosmograms signifying, roughly, the dissolution of all things into one another. They are metaphors for a state of ontological non-rigidity in which the identities of things are continually reprocessed through a single vast flowing continuum like Heraclitus's river. The individual identity of a part is submerged beneath the massive statement of the process as a whole. Schnabel's ground of broken shards comes from Pollock, but mediated by the discontinuous grounds of Rauschenberg's combines and collages, where separate entities momentarily form out of the flux of images, then break apart by its ambient surges and tugs. Schnabel's ground of shards is broken first, fluid second. Figures seen upon it are fragmented by the underlying brokenness of the ground of being. It is not a Modernist postulation of a whole and enduring selfhood that is presented in these works, but a feeling of fragmentation. The plate paintings are related, for instance, though with different feeling and tone, to Tony Cragg's use of fragments to build up decentred figures, or to Kounellis's use of fragments to suggest the brokenness of cultural norms in the late modern world.

But the significance of Schnabel's ceramic-shard ground goes beyond fragmentation. Lay one of these paintings down on the ground, rather than hanging it on the wall, and it ceases to be a painting and becomes a sculptural representation of an archaeological site, particularly of neolithic and bronze age sites which are characterized above all by the massing of broken ceramic shards sticking out of the ground at all angles. **The Mud in Mudanza** 1982 most directly and clearly conveys this content. The ground is itself an image. It is the loam of history that lies there among the gaping vessels that seem to come from another age. It is the dissolving and fertilizing ground of the past on which we raise our brief constructions, which are equally to be broken down into the death-and-life swamp of the archaeological rubbish dump. The themes that surge and flow through the tumultuous grounds are: history, the rise and fall of cultures, their relativity, time as seedbed of both past and future, the feeling of history flowing like a sewer, and so on. The fact that the shards are not really from ancient ceramic wares (though in some cases, like **The Mud in Mudanza,** they look that way) but contemporary ones, usually brand new from the stores and sometimes still bearing labels or price tags, focuses the onslaught of ravaging time onto our own moment. It is our own dream of history that is sinking into the broken scrap heap of the past before our eyes. Images that appear on such a screen are almost transparent. They seem to hover in front of the ground, already broken, scattered, decentred. They peer at us not as they were when they were themselves, but as the broken relics of selves that could not hold together through the storm of time, that were broken down in the crucible of nature to be reprocessed into other things. This, not heroic selfhood, is the basic ingredient of the iconography of the plate paintings.

There is a certain thoroughness to the relentless way this motif is worked out. **The Mud in Mudanza** presents the ground not as a bearer of an image or signifier, but as an image or signifier in itself. In **The Sea** 1981, the ground of broken crockery becomes a metaphor of itself. Time is presented as an ocean of ruins falling always from the past upon the present; it is an oceanic process without internal order or necessity, subject only to constant random reorderings like the reordering of flotsam with each tide or, more precisely, each wave. In the world's literature the sea is a traditional metaphor for the ground of being. Here the aliveness of the ground itself precedes any image upon it.

Despite imprecations of his images as disordered, meaningless, and purely gestural, Schnabel presents an iconography. It is not one that can be added up piece by piece, but one that works by a sense of superimpositions, restatements or semantic overlays of a small group of closely related concepts. The theme of the fragment redoubles itself through these layerings. In **Blue Nude with Sword** 1979, fragmentary classical columns torn out of their architectural setting restate the motif of the rise and fall of civilizations. The theme of the fragment appears in three layers: the ground, the representation of classical ruins, and the fact that the imagery itself is a quotational pastiche of historical fragments. The nude warrior poised on the two columns like a living sculpture is a figure from Pollaiuolo's *Battle of Naked Men.* The incense or oil-burning column is copied from a paper coffee cup. The merging of high and low cultural elements from different eras acts out the randomness of cultural dichotomies and sequences. Human selfhood falls to the passage of time as the blood-red head falls to the ground. The swordsman's apparent heroism is mocked by his placement on a sculpture pedestal: heroism is presented as an artifice. His is not a free, personal exercise of will; it is the process of time and change working through him. It is the violence that drives history, or is history, that sends the bloody head to the ground beneath the swordsman's strike as beneath the scythe of time.

Ancient philosophy featured the concept of a fecund metaphysical Oneness, or infinity, which was often pictured as a constantly moving self-adjusting oceanic abyss from which figures are thrown up momentarily like waves on a surface, then sink back through the law of time, which always balances the One, never giving out without taking back. This concept has also had a powerful presence in classical Modernist painting; it underlies the metaphysical monochrome tradition and is often involved in the related cult of the ground or surface. Pollock's allover ground expresses something like this; it asserts the primacy of the ground over the figure, or dissolves the figure into the ground. The figure is located within a flux which denies fixed representation. In the classic drip paintings Pollock shows us the oceanic ground alone, no figure rising from it or sinking into it. In the later paintings with implications of figuration, the flux seems to halt briefly and unpredictably before dissolving again. Schnabel's works are also involved with this concept, in the ground, in the iconography of the figures, and in the relation between figure and ground. The decaying and fertile archaeological-site ground is like the ocean of time from which the blue nude leaps into being and into which his adversary, balancing, falls.

These rudiments of an iconography were visible in Schnabel's work as early as 1975 and are unifying elements in the oeuvre as a whole. In the oil painting **Accatone** 1978, a broken classical statue is depicted on a column-like pedestal. The figure was mutilated at the moment, or in the act, of flexing its muscle and showing its strength. Its heroism is presented in the context of its own failure, its inability to remain unbroken by time. In **Head of Albert** 1980, a male human head and shoulders lie on the ground of broken ceramic as if sinking into it. The broken statue appears again in **Death of Fashion** 1978, **Procession (for Jean Vigo)** 1979, **Vallensasca, Italian Hero** 1978-79, and elsewhere. Sometimes, as in **The Bathers** 1980, and **St. Francis in Ecstasy** 1980, it is merely hinted at; always it is an active iconographic statement. Columns from classical ruins appear in **The Geography Lesson** 1981, and **Act of Faith** 1981, which includes a broken Ionic column capital and a small sculpture pedestal with a sculpture on it covered with a cloth an image from Max Beckmann. In **800 Blows** 1983, a classical head, based on the over lifesize conventional sculptures of the Roman emperor Constantine, lies atop a junkheap of broken shards. In **Cookie's Doll** 1984, a small bright-eyed mummy looks out from the archaeological ground. Many other works extend the theme.

There has of course been a surge of reprocessed classical imagery in recent art both in Europe and in America. The theme of the fragment dominates much of this work. One is reminded of the use of classical motifs as icons by Anton Raffael Mengs (1728-79) or of classical ruins by Giovanni Battista Piranesi (1720-78). There are interesting similarities and differences. In the eighteenth century, archaeology began to develop, and the art of the time reflected a growing fascination with it. In the twentieth century the motif is not about archaeology, the putting back together of fragments, but about deconstruction, about taking a culture apart or revealing it inwardly, as a ruin is laid bare to the eye. The eighteenth century was an age when democratic constitutions were written, always on the models of the Greeks and Romans. There was a sense of taking up the torch from the fallen civilization of the ancients. The need for the imagery of the classical ruin in our time, on the other hand, arises not from a sense of resuming where the Greeks left off, but from a sense that our own edifice may soon be a ruin. It is significant that both these are revolutionary ages when the future is like a deck of cards flung into the air. In the eighteenth century the advent of democracy and Romanticism was imminent; now the Post-Modern vista stretches undefined before us. The classical ruin is a kind of emblem, or negative emblem, of Modernism, prominent at its beginning and prominent again in this moment which has been heralded, perhaps prematurely, as its end. De Chirico used the motif of broken classical sculpture to express a haunting Romantic sense of a lost perfection which somehow was ourselves. Kounellis uses it more politically, to express both loss of cultural and personal wholeness, and the historical task of building a new whole again out of the fragments. These two artists, both Modernists, see history as having a direction, as departing from a primal perfection and heading towards an ultimate one. The fragment is, for them, not the great reality; the reality is the whole that is implied by the fragment, the whole vessel of which it was once a part, and which the archaeologist seeks to put back together again. For Schnabel, on the other hand, the ocean of fragments, without being put back together again, is already a whole; is itself a place, or a condition, for living (there is no past state in particular to lament or any future state to bend one's effort to attaining).

The sense of time or history as an ocean filled with the fragments of the past and randomly laying them on the beach of the present is duplicated at another level by the presence of quotational elements throughout the œuvre. In **Blue Nude,** as we have seen, the central figure is from a painting by Pollaiuolo, while the column-altar is from a paper cup of the 1980s. In **The Exile** 1980, the young man holding a basket of flowers is a copy of a figure in Carravaggio; the other figure is from a child's comic. In **Understanding Self-Hate** 1981, there is a face from an August Sander photograph. **Birthday** 1980, and **Pomme de Terre** 1980-1981, derive from the same children's book. **Act of Faith** 1981, contains an image from Max Beckmann. **Red Sky** 1984, and **Incantation** 1984, contain figures from Goya. The skull in **St. Francis in Ecstasy** 1980, is based on a El Greco painting. **Giacomo Expelled from the Temple** 1976-1978, is based on Giotto. Popular magazines provided images for **Ethnic Types No. 15 and No. 72** 1984, and **Ethnic Type No. 14** 1984. Courbet's head of Baudelaire appears in **Starting to Sing**

1981. There are elements of Ingres, Rodchenko, and others; Schnabel's imagery is, finally as quotational as that of the appropriators. His oeuvre as a whole is like the sea churning with fragments of the past, stirred up by the storm of the present. Nature is, similarly, a source of fragments and relics the antlers, the affixed timbers, roots, branches, pieces of animal hide, and so on, that coexist with the fragments of cultural images. Obviously Rauschenberg's example is relevant to these added sculptural elements, but they may also be found in Pollock, as in the hobby horse head affixed to the canvas *The Wooden Horse: Number 10A* 1948.

The motif of fragmentation redoubles or re-expresses itself again as does that of transparency and layering. Derived from the work of Picabia, this iconographic element has figured prominently in the New Painting of the eighties, in both Europe (Sigmar Polke, Anselm Kiefer, and others) and America (Schnabel, David Salle, and others). Most commonly it is human images that are layered by these artists, iconographically suggesting the multiplicity of modes of selfhood and the evanescence of human existence. Human identity is seen as lacking essence and coherence. Layered images from different ages or provenances depict the arbitrariness of historical sequence; each layer of the past is a transparency through which all others can be seen. This is a post-structuralist image that sees a self as a layering of different codes, changing as they shift their arrangement or as new ones are imprinted. In Schnabel's œuvre the layering of images has been especially associated with the paintings on velvet, tarpaulin, linoleum, and burlap. On these grounds, as on the ground of broken ceramics, the paint-drawn image tends to hover in front of the physical surface. In **Nicknames of Maitre d's** 1984, human types from various cultural zones are partially drawn. There is a Buddha-like figure with a topknot, a showgirl, an athlete, and others, layered around a coffin-like shape in the centre which shows signs of becoming a crucifix. The theme of the relativity of different types of humanity reappears in other velvet paintings, including **Ethnic Type No. 14** 1984 and **Ethnic Types No. 15 and No. 72** 1984, and in the plate painting with an image of an Australian aborigine, **Aborigine Painting** 1980. The tarpaulins, once used for covering trucks, are surfaces that already have a visual history before they are altered by the artist. The ground of stained cloth, with its real history of involvement in the world of labour, commerce, and the highway is, like the ground of shards, an analogue of the seedbed of history, the sedimentation of shape upon shape like generation upon generation. Schnabel treats these grounds as guides and emphasizes images that seem already suggested by them. Several works of 1986 are painted over

Kabuki theatre backdrops. As in the **Ethnic Types** and the **Aborigine Painting,** these works suggest a Post-Modern sense of the relativity of cultural and ethnic norms and the propriety of combining any of them in any way at all. Found grounds have been increasingly prominent in Schnabel's recent work. They indicate a certain relinquishing of total control, a mingling of self with other, and relate to such Post-Modern works as Maura Sheehan's windshield paintings (one of the rare similarities which Schnabel himself has remarked on).

The size of Schnabel's paintings has been steadily on the increase since the mid seventies. Like other elements of his work, it has frequently been denounced as constituting an heroic claim. But this reading is not consistent with his iconography as a whole. In context of his oeuvre, the expansive size of the work might better be understood as a signifier of the inclusive screen of nature, a miming of the way nature, like **The Sea,** makes a whole of many fragments within one embrace. There is also a desire to knit the work into surrounding space, in some cases by a prior history in the outside world, in others by an embracing scale, or by the presence of elements that enter the painting from outside it, cross it, then exit again. In **Pomme de Terre** 1980-81, over the ground of figures adopted from a children's book, an intrusive brown biomorphic shape moves across the canvas and out. It produces that layering of nature and culture that is one of the characteristic themes of the work. The brown biomorph wandering like a melon vine or a cancerous tumour across the page of the children's book is the sign of involvement in natural process, of the endless growth and change of things that will not stay still for human objects but will grow right over them as the mud of Mudanza grew over the civilization (ours) whose trace is barely seen beneath it.

The subjects of history and time lead to the subject of death. In this oeuvre the theme of death is confronted not so much in an attempt to stave off the moment of ruin and create something that will live on afterwards, as to mediate the fear of death by dealing with it on a metaphysical level as a component of the universal process of time. Coming to grips with death is coming to grips with nature. One function of the added animal materials is to reduce culture to a natural level where the theme of death becomes transparent. **Matador on a Stick** 1983, shows antlers growing from the matador's own head. Like the blue nude, he slays and he will be slain. His nature has the sacrificial beast in it, like the bull he sacrifices. The naturalness of death, its non-tragic and non-heroic character, is the subject also of the so-called medical paintings.

In **Avoiding Open Heart Surgery (Chest Cavity)** 1985, the heart, popularly the reservoir of human feeling, is seen as a purely animal thing having death as its nature or destiny. **Bob and Joe** 1984 presents two figures as enlarged, pumping organs with their arteries severed. In this complexity of motifs, history, time, and death appear as alternative ways of viewing the matrix of human life, the process in which it is located. Many of the loose biomorphic shapes in the abstract and semi-abstract paintings like the **Mutant King,** belong in this genre. The king, of course, is a traditional symbol of the ongoing birth-death process ('the king is dead, long live the king'). **The King of the Wood** 1984, is based on a passage of Sir James Frazer's classic work about the ritual linkage of life and death, *The Golden Bough.* The passage describes an ancient ritual kingship in which each king is killed from ambush by the person who will succeed him, in a chain going indefinitely backwards and forwards through history, even, in a sense, comprising history.

Pagan sacrificial imagery converts, in the paintings of the eighties, to related elements of Christian imagery. The change does not alter the content, but the feeling in which it is expressed. The sense that humanity belongs to nature by the fact, almost the gift, of sharing mortality with other natural beings, is portrayed now with a certain sacramental sheen. Modernist art for at least a generation has lacked overt Christian imagery. Around mid-century there was a general assumption, in line with the Modernist feeling that history moves inexorably onward, that this subject matter could not be painted anymore, though it could still enter into titles of works, such as Newman's *Stations of the Cross.* Schnabel's selection of this body of imagery is typically ambiguous. From a Post-Modern point of view it is reasonable to revive any imagery from the past, and the fact that no one else revived this one is strangely telling about the hidden linkage between Christianity and Romanticism, which are bound by their devotion to the sublime, among other things. Christian iconography has not yet been reduced by Post-Modern quotational parody; it is in a sense still too hot to handle in that way. In Schnabel's work the Christian imagery, like the relation with Pollock, seems to appear not with ironic distance so much as with a sense of personal continuity. The Christianity expressed in these works is of a pantheistic type somewhat like that of Robert Bresson in works like *Au Hazard Balthazar,* where the Christ presence is shown as a force pervading nature. The sacrament of communion is seen as a thing that is going on constantly through all of nature, even, consciously or not, through all of culture, which is a part of nature. The Christ nature dies in each thing that dies, and so on. Everyday events attain a sacramental status that heightens their availability to feeling, somewhat as in certain areas of Greek paganism, Hinduism, and other non-dualistic religions. **Vita** 1984 extends into the Christian sacramental format the presence of the goddesses of pre-Christian religions. The female Christ echoes Carl Dreyer's cinematic extension of the Christ nature to Joan and to her portrayer, Falconetti. **Vita** evokes nature as a universal female principle undergoing the sacrament of sacrifice and death everywhere all the time. As in the plate paintings, the figure restates with an altered tonality what the archaeological-site ground has already stated beneath it. As the earth filled with shards (the mud of Mudanza) is a fertile swampy place where things sink in and rise again in different forms, so the goddess hanging on the tree or cross is nature constantly recycling its forces and appearances through a process like death and birth at once. The vision of nature as a vast sacred process yielding up forms and taking them down again is transposed into an allegory of painting in **Veronica's Veil** 1984, where the cloth imprinted with the face of Christ is an analogue of the painted fabric. The process of art-making is seen as a part of the vast natural activity of cycling and recycling forms. Nature in this formulation functions as time did in the classical paintings. It is, in effect, deified. This area of Schnabel's work – its pantheistic enthusiasm presented through a mixture of pagan and Christian images, and its symbolic incorporation of painting into a death and fertility cult – relates, among classical Modernist forebears, to Picasso. In the charnel house/temple in *Guernica,* for example, war is portrayed as a part of an ongoing sacrificial rite that is the negative aspect of the process of nature.

Before 1975 Schnabel's work involved elementary diagrammatic symbols of various kinds. It moved through a phase of Greco-Roman classical symbols into a phase of Christian symbols, and recently Jewish symbols have begun to appear. This unpremeditated process reflects a Post-Modern desire to incorporate history, to relive it in one's own person. What is Post-Modern in this impulse is its hidden implication that history is over – a theme that was vividly spelled out in Pat Steir's *Breughel: A Vanitas of Style.* When history ends it is not so much the past that is over as the future. The past is never over and always beginning. Altering the model of history creates the past anew.

Schnabel's iconography does not bespeak the unreconstructed Modernist self-image. The content of his paintings has more to do with the work of Post-Moderns who have emphasized the fragmented nature of things, such as Steir and Cragg, than with Modernists of fragmentation, such as the Chirico and Kounellis. On the other hand, his desire to carry forward the expressiveness of Picasso or Pollock suggests a Modernist sense of continuity with mainstream art history. This ambiguity is not unusual. It is found in Sherri Levine's recent switch from quotational paintings to abstract paintings of her own. It is found in the work of many artists, such as Joseph Glasco, Ross Bleckner, and others, with whom Schnabel feels a connection. Schnabel's mixing of Neo-Expressionism and appropriation is a picture of our communal psyche at this moment. In a sense this is the main point to attend to.

       The Modern/Post-Modern antinomy has grown into a new kind of dualism: either the Neo-Expressionists are right and the appropriators wrong, or vice versa. The Post-Modern project of undermining Modernist absolutism has confusedly become another absolutism. But to allow Modernism and Post-Modernism to be polarized as a new ethical dualism is to misunderstand the needs of the moment. What is needed is not a new puritanism but a flexible continuum on which Modernism and Post-Modernism may approach one another. The overthrow of the past is precisely a Modernist obsession. Post-Modernism cannot be obsessed with the overthrow of Modernism without becoming a repressed form of it. Relating to the past means a complex balancing of various probabilities. If these do not include threads of positive connection, the deconstructive impulse, in its nihilistic dream of ground-zero, becomes another attempt to return to Eden.

       A parable may speak more clearly. It is told in the Pali suttas that the Buddha taught to all who inquired the doctrine of the unreality of the self. One day a visitor asked if this not-self was a dogma with him. He replied, 'Not at all. I teach not-self because everyone who comes to me already believes self. If you came to me believing not-self, I would teach you the self.'

Ornamental Despair (Painting for Ian Curtis), 1980
Oil on velvet
229 x 427
Saatchi Collection, London

Catalogue

Dimensions are given in centimetres, height before width

Jack the Bellboy, 'A Season in Hell', 1975
Oil, joint compound and pencil on canvas
183 × 122
Arthur and Carol Goldberg Collection, New York

Giacomo Expelled from the Temple, 1976-78
Oil and wax on canvas
231 × 212
Lannan Foundation, Venice, California

Painting for Aldo Moro, 1978
Oil and wax on canvas
213 × 188
Gerald Just, Hannover

The Patients and the Doctors, 1978
Plaster, oil, plates and tile on masonite
244 × 274
Julian Schnabel, New York

St. Sebastian – Born in 1951, 1979
Oil and wax on canvas
282 × 168
Julian Schnabel, New York

Procession (for Jean Vigo), 1979
Oil and wax on canvas
279 × 218
Private collection

Circumnavigating the Sea of Shit, 1979
Plates, oil and wax on masonite
244 × 244
Galerie Bruno Bischofberger, Zürich

Aborigine Painting, 1980
Oil, plates, bondo, wood and canvas
244 × 213
Jacqueline Schnabel, New York

The Geography Lesson, 1980
Oil on velvet
244 × 213
Galerie Bruno Bischofberger, Zürich

Exile, 1980
Oil and antlers on wood
229 × 305
Barbara and Eugene M. Schwartz, New York

Ornamental Despair (Painting for Ian Curtis), 1980
Oil on velvet
229 × 427
Saatchi Collection, London

Pomme de Terre, 1980-81
Oil and wax on canvas
229 × 213
Private collection

Prehistory: Glory, Honor, Privilege, Poverty, 1981
Oil and antlers on pony skin
325 × 450
Saatchi Collection, London

The Sea, 1981
Oil, plates, antler and plaster on wood; charred wood
274 × 396
Saatchi Collection, London

Mutant King, 1981
Oil and wax on tarpaulin
274 × 366 (from the five-part work 'The Mutant Kings' 1981)
Private collection

Portrait of God, 1981
Oil and wax on tarpaulin
274 × 366 (from the five-part work 'The Mutant Kings' 1981)
Private collection

Rest, 1982
Oil on wood supported by beam
427 × 488
Saatchi Collection, London

The Mud in Mudanza, 1982
Oil, plates and bondo on wood
274 × 579
Julian Schnabel, New York

Maria Callas No. 2, 1982
Oil on velvet
274 × 305
Private collection

Maria Callas No. 4, 1982
Oil on velvet
274 × 305
Saatchi Collection, London

Portrait of J.S. in Hakodate, Japan, 1934, 1983
Oil and fibreglass on tarpaulin
290 × 396
Musée National d'Art Moderne, Centre Georges Pompidou, Paris

St. Patrick, 1983
Oil and fibreglass on tarpaulin
290 × 396
Private collection, courtesy The Pace Gallery, New York

Memory and Stimulus for Memory (The Marriage of Mary Boone and Michael Werner), 1983
Oil and fibreglass on tarpaulin
290 × 396
Saatchi Collection, London

Griddle, 1983
Oil and fibreglass on tarpaulin
335 × 244
Janet Green Collection, London

A.D. (Wreath for Tennessee Williams), 1983
Oil and fibreglass on tarpaulin
335 × 244
Saatchi Collection, London

Vita, 1983
Oil, bondo and plates on wood
305 × 305
Private collection, courtesy The Pace Gallery, New York

Ethnic Types No. 15 and No. 72, 1984
Oil, animal hide and modelling paste on velvet
274 × 305
Private collection, courtesy The Pace Gallery, New York

Some Peaches (Sebastian's Summer Poem), 1984
Oil and modelling paste on velvet
305 x 274
Mr. and Mrs. Robert Kaye, New Jersey

Resurrection: Albert Finney meets Malcolm Lowry, 1984
Oil and modelling paste on velvet
305 x 274
Julian Schnabel, New York

Salinas Cruz, 1984
Oil and modelling paste on velvet
274 x 305
Speyer Family Collection, New York

The Walk Home, 1985
Oil, plates, copper, bronze and fibreglass on bondo
284 x 589
Aron and Phyllis Katz Collection, Colorado

The Trial, 1985
Oil and modelling paste on tarpaulin
279 x 538
Private collection

Prison: Waiting for an Ultraviolet Ray, 1985
Oil and fibreglass on linoleum
366 x 571
Janet Green Collection, London

Rebirth III – The Red Box (painted after the death of Joseph Beuys), 1986
Oil and tempera on muslin
376 x 340
Private collection

Jack the Bellboy, 'A Season in Hell', 1975
Oil, joint compound and pencil on canvas
183 x 122
Arthur and Carol Goldberg Collection, New York

Giacomo Expelled from the Temple, 1976-78
Oil and wax on canvas
231 x 212
Lannan Foundation, Venice, California

The Patients and the Doctors, 1978
Plaster, oil, plates and tile on masonite
244 x 274
Julian Schnabel, New York

St. Sebastian – Born in 1951, 1979
Oil and wax on canvas
282 × 168
Julian Schnabel, New York

Procession (for Jean Vigo), 1979
Oil and wax on canvas
279 × 218
Private collection

Circumnavigating the Sea of Shit, 1979
Plates, oil and wax on masonite
244 x 244
Galerie Bruno Bischofberger, Zürich

Aborigine Painting, 1980
Oil, plates, bondo, wood and canvas
244 x 213
Jacqueline Schnabel, New York

The Geography Lesson, 1980
Oil on velvet
244 x 213
Galerie Bruno Bischofberger, Zürich

Exile, 1980
Oil and antlers on wood
229 × 305
Barbara and Eugene M. Schwartz, New York

Pomme de Terre, 1980-81
Oil and wax on canvas
229×213
Private collection

Prehistory: Glory, Honor, Privilege, Poverty, 1981
Oil and antlers on pony skin
325 × 450
Saatchi Collection, London

The Sea, 1981
Oil, plates, antler and plaster on wood; charred wood
274×396
Saatchi Collection, London

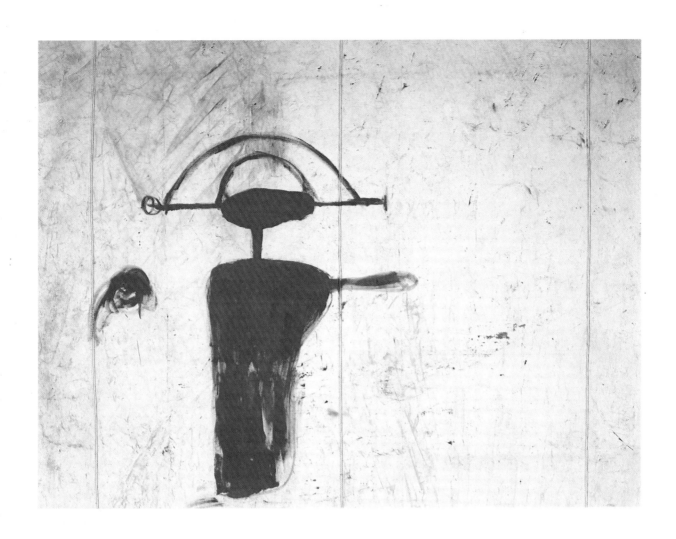

Mutant King, 1981
Oil and wax on tarpaulin
274 × 366 (from the five-part work 'The Mutant Kings' 1981)
Private collection

Portrait of God, 1981
Oil and wax on tarpaulin
274 × 366 (from the five-part work 'The Mutant Kings' 1981)
Private collection

Rest, 1982
Oil on wood supported by beam
427 × 488
Saatchi Collection, London

The Mud in Mudanza, 1982
Oil, plates and bondo on wood
274 × 579
Julian Schnabel, New York

Maria Callas No. 2, 1982
Oil on velvet
274 × 305
Private collection

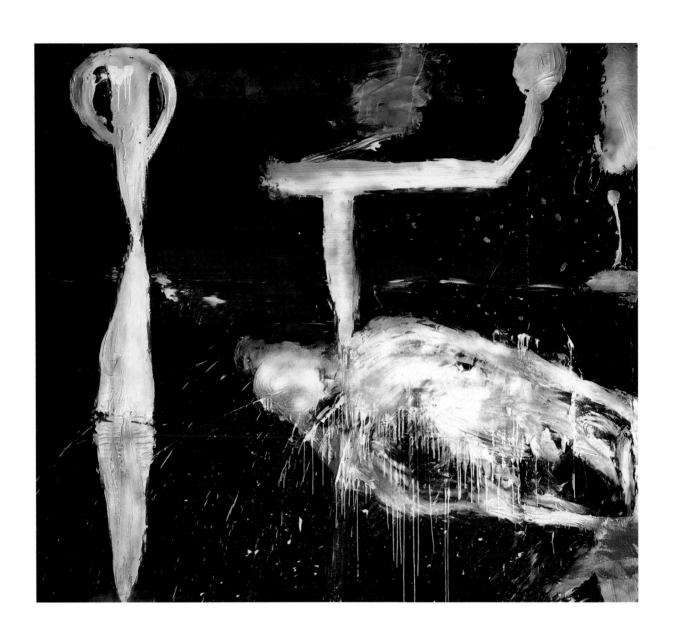

Maria Callas No. 4, 1982
Oil on velvet
274 x 305
Saatchi Collection, London

Portrait of J.S. in Hakodate, Japan, 1934, 1983
Oil and fibreglass on tarpaulin
290×396
Musée national d'art moderne, Centre Georges Pompidou, Paris

St. Patrick, 1983
Oil and fibreglass on tarpaulin
290×396
Private collection

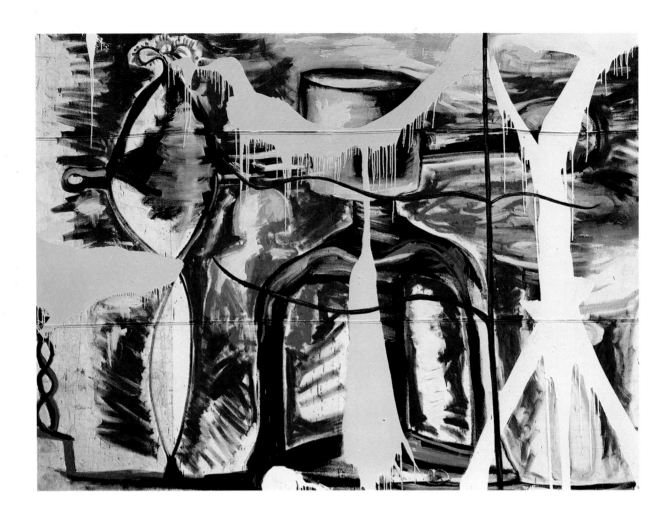

Memory and Stimulus for Memory (The Marriage of Mary Boone and Michael Werner), 1983
Oil and fibreglass on tarpaulin
290×396
Saatchi Collection, London

Griddle, 1983
Oil and fibreglass on tarpaulin
335 × 244
Janet Green Collection, London

A.D. (Wreath for Tennessee Williams), 1983
Oil and fibreglass on tarpaulin
335 x 244
Saatchi Collection, London

Vita, 1983
Oil, bondo and plates on wood
305 × 305
Private collection

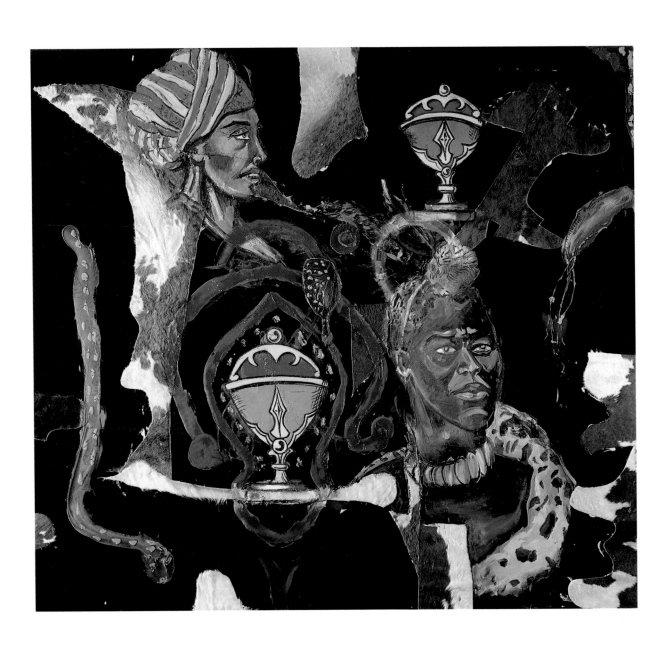

Ethnic Types No. 15 and No. 72, 1984
Oil, animal hide and modelling paste on velvet
274×305
Private collection

Some Peaches (Sebastian's Summer Poem), 1984
Oil and modelling paste on velvet
305 x 274
Mr. and Mrs. Robert Kaye, New Jersey

Resurrection: Albert Finney meets Malcolm Lowry, 1984
Oil and modelling paste on velvet
305 × 274
Julian Schnabel, New York

Salinas Cruz, 1984
Oil and modelling paste on velvet
274 x 305
Speyer Family Collection, New York

The Walk Home, 1985
Oil, plates, copper, bronze and fibreglass on bondo
284 x 589
Aron and Phyllis Katz Collection, Colorado

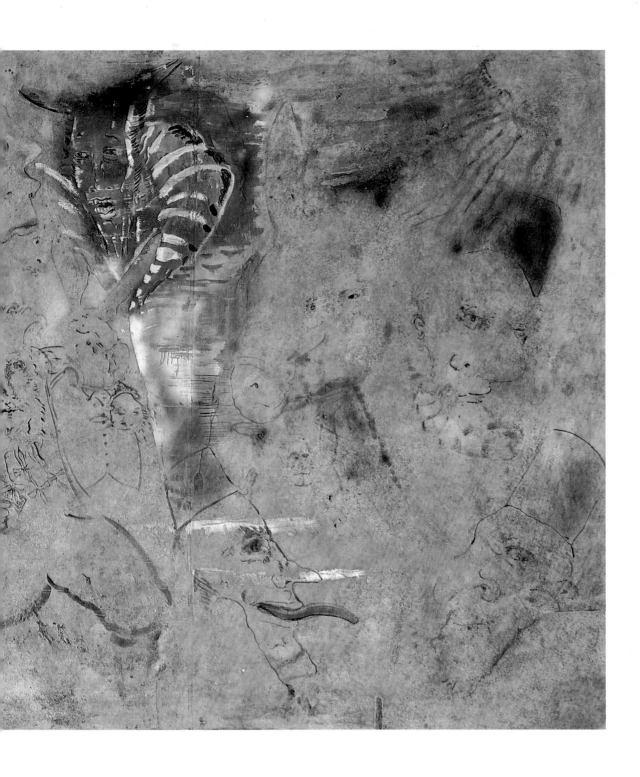

The Trial, 1985
Oil and modelling paste on tarpaulin
279×538
Private collection

Prison: Waiting for an Ultraviolet Ray, 1985
Oil and fibreglass on linoleum
366 × 571
Janet Green Collection, London

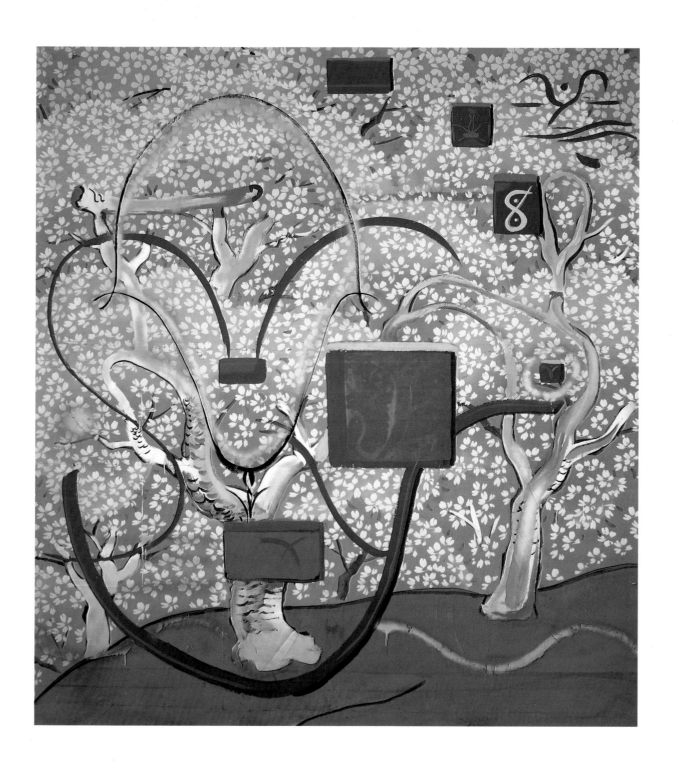

Rebirth III, The Red Box (painted after the death of Joseph Beuys), 1986
Oil and tempera on muslin
376 × 340
Private collection

Julian Schnabel
in conversation with
Matthew Collings

Your work is sometimes compared to current European art and in particular the art of Polke, Kiefer, Joseph Beuys...

We're all part of one world of art. Let's be clear about something – Beuys has been a great inspiration to me. He was Polke's and Kiefer's teacher. Polke was a friend of mine before I had ever seen a painting of his. We met in 1974 in New York. People are always setting up competitions unnecessarily. Why should Kiefer and I, for instance, be pitted against each other? Of course there has been an exchange of ideas. I think Polke, Kiefer and I all got something from Beuys, in that Beuys presented an alternative to the esoteric trappings of art and this notion of its progressiveness. He was able to make an art that was outside the formal realm – he put it on a generic, humanistic level. So things like theatricality, illustration, which had been dirty words in America, things alluding to life, which had been excluded from the forum of art in Clement Greenberg's idea of it, and in the American chauvinism of that time, became part of the possibility of art through Beuys.

A lot of people here viewed Polke as a failed

European Pop artist, which he was in a way. He may have failed at Pop art but he didn't fail at *his* art. The things that kept him from fitting into Pop art are what makes him a distinctive artist now. Whatever his reasons, he was equipped with an attitude that freed him from the boundaries of what Pop art was about. Finally what he was doing had to do with notating inarticulateness – something that can be sensed but which you can't quite put your finger on; what I call the texture of poverty. I think in Polke's paintings there's a poetic configuration that transcends the imagery of the work, or the way it's made, and which operates almost as a spirit.

Would you like to think of your own work in that way?

I do. If it wasn't in my work I wouldn't see it in his. The poetic I'm talking about has to do with a configuration that exists in Kiefer, in Francesco Clemente, and I think it exists in my work. Our work is very different in many ways but in all of it there's a feeling that these things were in the world already and that they were deformed.

Reproduced, by kind permission, from *Artscribe International*, September/October 1986

The paintings are deformed?

All these paintings are about a recognition. They aren't pure in the sense that they've just come out of somebody's imagination. They're affected by some kind of unnameable pressure that is part of reality. It's part of a theatre of things. It has to do with the way the trees look – the bark on the trees, things on the land, the way the beach looks. Things we know already.

European artists sometimes say your work is 'Americanized' European art – European ideas through Frank Stella...

What in the world does Frank Stella's work have to do with mine? I used to be criticized in America for being too European. I don't know what European tendency we're talking about...in the sense of French paintings *vis-à-vis* Picasso, or the current idea of the 'collective-subjective', which is a different point...?

I think when people compare your work with Polke they think of the difference in terms of the presentation of the object, in that post-war American tradition that Frank Stella epitomizes.

Well, his work isn't perverse enough... and I don't think I'm a *little* more perverse than Frank Stella and if I were *really* perverse then I'd be a European...I would say the possibilities of freedom are no different here in America than in Europe. I guess anybody can paint any way they like, all over the world, until they're stopped by force. (Genet wrote *Our Lady of the Flowers* in prison – twice, because they threw it away the first time.) But a lot of Europeans come here so that they can be free of their historical baggage – I mean socially. The world cannot afford all these cultural distinctions. There's only one bomb, it'll get my kids, Francesco's and Kiefer's.

How do you like Baselitz?

René Ricard said in 1981 that my art was about 'freemasonry in art'. I hate to disappoint him...I could sit here and put down every artist in the world because I could find something wrong with all of them. I could find something wrong with Francesco Clemente and he's one of my favourites – but why should I when I love his paintings? Why should I say that Baselitz is a provincial painter? He is, and his paintings are great. I prefer some of them to Bill de Kooning's. If I think of Kiefer or of Francesco, I think of them finding something that's already in the world and then

working on top of that thing, dealing with it. I think it's more a generational than a national issue. Beuys really gave birth to this idea.

How can you qualify the idea of neo-expressionism without talking about 'neo' or a rehash of something?

I don't want to qualify it at all. I think 'neo' or 'post' – these are just journalists' words. I don't think about neo-expressionism, it doesn't exist. I'm a modern artist.

Why do you think there is so much more acceptance in America for Kiefer than for Beuys?

Unfortunately people have a very conservative attitude towards art and they can digest a painted thing – whether it has straw or plates on it, they can find a place in their home to entertain this kind of art. But Beuys made some things that they didn't know what to do with. They sometimes weren't even things, they wouldn't even last. But I think you can find the written word and the pictoriality of Beuys in Kiefer's work. I understand why there has been so much more acceptance in America for Kiefer. It has to do with timing and this notion of the redeemed, cleansed guilt. It's like an agreement... it reminds me of the Bob Dylan song:

> Even though in the ovens six millions they fried
> Now even the Germans have God on their side

I think Kiefer is too accepting of his own myth.

How do you avoid that?

Well, I'm too screwed up to copy myself. I've got these things prepared to work on out back, and I don't know what the hell I'm going to do next. And my friends have been acting a little funny lately...

What does freedom mean in your work?

I once said that style is the fringe benefit of intention. I think you do something in a certain way – like the way you put on your shirt – and out of the involvement with materials you find that different alternatives present themselves. So 'freedom' is seeing the possibilities in many different things. Everyone is looking for some way to continue. And maybe their way is to notice the same thing over and over – the artist re-illustrating some idea that they already had for their audience. It's like getting paid to stop thinking – I don't think that's freedom. Freedom is being able to hang yourself with nobody worrying about it. For example, nobody asked me to make these new Japanese paintings. I have no idea if anyone will like them and I don't really care. That means my financial situation might go down and maybe my whole life will fall apart. But maybe I'm so arrogant and so stupid and have such a very bad idea of reality that rather than trying to placate, or second guess, an audience – or trying to fit into the artworld – I'd rather try to notice something out in the world that affects me and will make me do something that I wasn't already expecting to see. And in the end it doesn't really have anything to do with me – in the most selfish way it's just me wanting to make something that I can look at. I don't want that thing to be an illustration of my intelligence, or my aura, or my ego.

Many artists now are making a kind of critical work that seems to address the ironies of the commercial situation, and the situation of the work of art which has become just another commodity. For example, Sherri Levine…

Well, you could say I'm making these very large paintings that couldn't fit into anybody's home and which I can't sell, so therefore I have a very negative attitude towards the market. But I know that isn't true. I paint the paintings that size because that's the way I see them. I find the idea of making art about the art market very boring. For example when I made that painting in 1981 called *OK*, which was based on an Oskar Kokoschka poster, or the painting that looked like a Rodchenko – where I used a Rodchenko as a model for my own painting – I was just saying that anything can be a model. Something that exists, that you've seen – your wife maybe, or a tree, or something from a textbook – anything. I was just starting from the beginning. But I didn't make those paintings to say, 'Look, I can sell this painting, which is an image of another painting', it was just saying that anything can feed a work of art. For me, art is consciousness – it's a physical manifestation of a recognition. Different types of art address different things, some of the issues people address their art to I find completely uninteresting. I don't find art interesting that illustrates a Marxist concept about products. So even though I think she's a very intelligent artist, I find Sherri Levine's work uninteresting. The interesting thing about art is that as you make something it changes you. I'm interested in something that changes my preconceptions; either it transcends the material it's made of, or it makes me feel altered in some way. I even think that while Sherri was making these pictures of other pictures and just presenting them like that, that the making of them actually changed her.

The paintings became *her* paintings and even though she had her pose of criticality and distance and was 'responsible', she was still affected by what she was doing. The notion of making art and not being affected by it is just a lie. She once picked on me for being optimistic but I heard lately that she's started painting and has become optimistic herself…

You don't subscribe to the idea of distance, of critical control?

Whether you're putting some paint on a piece of canvas or just glueing something down and not making any marks at all, or whether you're just selecting something to present – we're still talking about the quality of involvement, the artist's involvement with this thing that they select to do with their life.

Whenever I talk about these things I return to Beuys. I felt that he made his work to effect some kind of noticing of something that we're all a part of. He was talking about some kind of collective consciousness, not about the aesthetic glorification of an object – maybe it was in its most modest and truest sense. Beuys's work is useful. Even if I may love to look at the paintings I make – and I do covet them, my real pleasure in them is that, for me, the work manifests a kind of love that I find impossible with another person, but which I can put into these paintings, so that it becomes a kind of love note to someone who isn't even born yet; and I feel satisfied accepting my role as a dead person when I do that.

Everyone tries to second guess your reasons for doing something and they make connections: you make something and at the time the work appears to be like other things. Artists make things and the things start to constitute the history of objects and once that occurs different artists' works mark points of convergence and so people will say that something looks a bit like Arshile Gorky or Cy Twombly or someone else. But the reasons why it looks that way have to do with biological need, or the generic potentiality of those forms for humans. So this lame iconographical way of looking – 'this came from that' doesn't contribute to anything. For example, a critic who doesn't deserve to be mentioned looked at my painting of St Francis and said that the image came from Bellini. In fact it came from a picture of an Ethiopian in *National Geographic*. The skull didn't even look like Bellini – it was better than Bellini, it was El Greco! I'm not afraid to look like somebody else but the audience, or the critic or whoever, has to look for the use that the artist has for all these things within their own work. And *that* makes up the language, not the critic's ability to say that something looks like a Franz Kline…

How competitive are you? It's supposed to be an American preoccupation…

It sounds like an English preoccupation to me since you're asking the question – maybe it's an art preoccupation. But even though you're leading me into this, I will be as dumb as possible and answer: Picasso is the best. I don't think it's an American preoccupation. An artist has to think that they're the best, even if they're lying to themselves. Was anyone as good as Picasso? Was he better than Braque or Juan Gris or Matisse – he thought Matisse was better. Was he better than Mondrian? And Mondrian was really good – was *he* better than Malevich? Can you tell, when you see the two rooms at the Stedelijk museum? People everywhere get angry about these judgements. If someone says I'm good then someone else thinks it must mean that Howard Hodgkin is bad, or not good enough.

Well, it's hard to compare Beuys with Picasso.

I don't think so. If we believe in art then we believe in art's legacy and the continuation of certain behaviour. And because the behaviour of Beuys, and the things he made, were so different in appearance to what had gone before, he extended the possibilities of art, particularly at a point where it was turning in on itself and becoming more artifact than art. He started to rekindle this possibility which had been a very intrinsic part of the modernist optimism and which was being ignored because of stylistic prejudices and the art policies of the time. I like to think that with Beuys – even though he started making work in the fifties when there was a lot of other work being made in America and a lot of older American artists wouldn't see it the same way I do – with him came the possibility of making work that could look completely different from Picasso, and for that reason would actually be an extension of Picasso. Picasso is the definition of modern. And I think my paintings are an extension of Picasso. There are attitudes in Picasso which I believe because I am a modern artist. I understand the logic of his late paintings. I understand what art meant to him. But I think it would be unfair not to mention Beuys in the same breath. A lot of Americans still don't understand that it was Beuys who instigated this current shift in art. They think it came from reductivism and minimalism and painting being dead and then resurrected – but I'm talking about an involvement with materials. The issue of whether it's a sculpture or a painting is obsolete, as well as the difference between figuration and abstraction. Even an artist like Jeff Koons has to begin again when everything else is over.

To take an object like a refrigerator and stick it on the wall is not a reductivist action, it's not minimalist – it has to do with the metaphoric power of materials. Even if the materials are manufactured, or they look new, the work has to do with the alchemic and accumulative power of these isolated objects. Even someone like Don Judd somehow believed that – even if he himself wouldn't acknowledge it.

What possesses anyone to make anything? They want to do something with themselves. Artists make things and then they find other things in the world that agree with the things they made, in an anterior agreement. For me that's the interesting thing. I don't really read about art… you need to forget all those things that you know and then look at something you've made and maybe see something different in it. I'll see a little Magritte perhaps, or a little Picabia here and there, or this and that. But the reason why these things are good is that they're part of our consciousness as modern, urban people. So freedom is in the commonality of language – and through that commonality somebody like Picasso could bend things around so you could see a diagrammatic x-ray of a sense of humour, or a mistake. That's what we find fascinating. To the critics in England who look to see how well drawn something is – well, it's also interesting to see how something can be disassembled, or how something can be absent in a painting, and you can get a sense of loss, or of longing from it.

Perhaps we should wind up with a last word on Europe…

We never left Europe! European painters accept the notion of imagery. They accept an image painted onto a rectangle. Americans needed to break it down so that there was a receiver for the image to be painted on. If I think of Lüpertz or Baselitz in the 1970s I think of their work as quite regressive, reactionary, 'homey'. Most of the other German work of the time was very influenced by American art and had become very didactic and boring. But the work that was neither of these, somehow was an informed work which at the same time couldn't care less about American chauvinism. Blinky Palermo couldn't care about it. He liked Ellsworth Kelly but he had a romantic belief in the anonymity of abstract art. And actually if you look at his drawings, they look a lot like Beuys. Why in the world would somebody believe that they could make their own art and it still resemble someone else's and still be OK? It has to do with a heavily romantic idea about the haunting ability of art, a belief in something that goes outside of the object, outside of the artist. It resides in the desire to see.

Writings by Julian Schnabel

I wanted to say something about how the image of a painting comes in and out of your own vision, your own ability to grasp it and use it and how sometimes you just can't work anymore; you can't. Something is exhausted and you can't pay attention anymore. You have the will to make something, but your wrists have gone dead on you. You go back and forth between having a lot of energy and stamina, feeling very equipped to do it; and other days it's all you can do to draw a circle, and you are interested in looking at a circle. You don't want to look at something that looks like a landscape, or a crucifix, or a beach, or anything; you want everything to become something else; you look forward instead of backwards. I don't want to look back but sometimes one has to, in their work, just to keep going. You look back at everything. I'm saying one thing and then I'm saying the exact opposite; both are true.

It's not expressionism, it is feelings that are important, not necessarily my feelings.

25 August 1981
First published in *Julian Schnabel,* Tate Gallery, 1982

I wonder what purpose, if any, possesses an artist to make things?

Agony has many faces: violent, passive, loud or quiet, making possible readings that go forwards and backwards in time (marking a specific moment). Pictures made to be scrutinized separately, but always as a part (good period, bad one) of the whole that makes up the body of work that stands as the artist's attitude towards life.

This is important because if we believe that we are free to act, then we are not restricted to creating structures that always have a similar appearance (commonly called style), or bound by our own past to always work in a style dictated by that which preceded.

Works must describe themselves, the world, and their inner need to exist in a specific way. I suggest that style is the effect or character, armed with intensity, a sense of purpose, a method, a syntax that reveals the will and need to make something. Style is the fringe benefit of intention and action completed.

In my painting it is only that. It is not about style, not about other styles; style is available, depending on the demands and needs of a particular work. A painting can proceed from one's inspiration and be complete and successful in the sense that the need is materialized, the revelation realized. It may, at the same time, be inaccessible to the public addressed; for a time inaccessible to everybody.

For an artist in my position all (the public) is an unlikely number to understand my work since so few are free enough of preconceptions to see what is there. To see what is there takes real interest on the part of the viewer.

Presenting a work publicly invites its own situation; that of emanating information with its very own specific qualities and viewing time; the possibility of a direct relationship, one to one, between the viewer and the object, is an ideal rarely achieved; there are so many distractions.

People have a funny involvement with art. They are interested in it for many reasons that address their relationship to the world: what art means to them; their idea of what it means to others; their conception of the artist's intent; and, perhaps lastly, how they actually feel about it. Layer upon layer, obscuring a direct relationship with the object.

There is altogether too much mediating going on; too many words and ideas and theories come between the viewer and the object of contemplation. On the spot digestion and 'interpretation' of a work of art by a critic/reporter, quick and witty reportage, serves to obfuscate meaning, as do the self-promotion of gallerists and the prestige and monetary interests of collectors, all riding on the back of the 'unseen' undigested work itself, veiled as it is in so many ways. The artist is not guiltless in all this; the economic support structure and the artist's dependence on it are constructed and inherited and not amenable to simplistic adjustment.

But this economic aspect is a separate issue from the artist's intention as realized in his work. And there is definitely a distinction between an artist and his work.

How, then, is the viewer supposed to have a direct relationship with a work of art? How to filter out all the distractions, to arrive at its true nature – the mentality, sensibility and history embodied and revealed in the work?

This brings us to the problem of incongruity. I no longer expect people to understand me. I no longer expect my work to be understood as I understand it.

Time seems to be an issue: the time in which a work exists; its own lifetime; the life of the artist. One might say that the artist's ecstasy, the relation in the realization of his intention in the successful work have only a tangential relationship to the art itself, but I maintain that is disputable. The artist feels deeply the need for personal agreement –

identity – between his intention and the result. Alive in the world he feels the natural need to live with others, to communicate something. The notion is one of making something, not for an audience, but with an awareness of the audience, some of whom are certainly not yet alive. The artist is necessarily involved with the idea of history, past and future. It is this chain of life, of objects made by artists, that I believe to be the artist's confidante and consolation within the quiet isolation that is the space created by art's incongruity to life; we live always with the absence of an immediate and easily available resolution of that incongruity. We are doomed to facile acceptance and dismissal of new and profound reifications of sense, history and feeling.

The true subject is meaning.

The description of the meaning of the work of art, the meaning to the artists who create them, the meaning of others' interpretations and what they have and do not have to do with the meaning (intention) of the work.

This meaning is my interest because it is my deepest desire for others to get the meaning of my work; nothing else, nothing less.

Only through the work can there be a recognition, a harmony of intention an revelation, artist and viewer communing. Making art is the only way some kinds of people mediate the world. It is the way they fit into the world. The work is ultimately a physical fact, a microcosm of the world for the artist, a handbook for others. It can only be constructed out of displaced love; the curiosity to know something (through the making) that is seemingly unknowable. Out of the acceptance of the finite terms (possibilities) of painting one achieves a self-respect. Through making objects one learns things about life that cannot be learned (or communicated) in any other way. It gets made out of the need for a direct, concrete truth that stays intact, available, as long as the work exists. It is a way of transgressing death. It reassures others of a stability, a sameness, a quality that is a recognition of a shared humanness and thought.

The materiality of a work of art is important only as long as its imparts a quality of being, meaning, feeling, a recognition. It is appropriate only as long as it is true; it is modern only so long as it is true. Deeper than conversation, it has its own dignity.

Authorship and ownership of an idea or work are not identical. The artist creates a symbiotic relationship of author and sign, handmade, a gift to others to align himself with them in a common truth; a clearer realization of the world we live in, an individual attempt to cut out the static, the shit.

All components of the work are parts of a desire

to transform the spirit; prior meanings, existing meanings, and newly attached meanings, all necessary to create in the work an accumulative meaning whose configuration is something no one has ever seen before. This doesn't mean you can't recognize it when you see it.

What artists can give to others, how they are of use in this life, is in their discovery of a point of convergence where the psysical fact denotes a state of consciousness.

This is how art is generative.

4 April 1983

The other day I was one of a group of artists Analee Newman, Barnett Newman's wife, had invited to her home. There were some inspired Barnett Newman paintings there. They weren't beautiful in the sense of luscious masterfully painted incidents. Their beauty was the trace of an investigation into a visual analog for freedom. They were a palimpsest, a collection of signals that triggered an emotional and an intellectual vision that resides in and outside of the painting.

There was one little painting with a green mottled surface and a yellow triangle, a vector painted on one side, and an orange line that stopped in the middle of the painting on the opposite side. The yellow went to the bottom, sitting in the picture in an awkward way. You notice yourself noticing the moment where the orange line stops in the middle of the painting. The quality of where the line stops on the colored ground isolates itself as the artist's selected act.

There was another painting on the same wall and it had a kind of a tannish, milky tan ground, with little flecks of burnt sienna in it and three yellowish blurs sort of rubbed into it, even though it was a relatively homogeneous surface. It looked like plywood. It didn't look like plywood. It also looked like deep space, things floating in a landscape. Right next to that on the same panel was one line, a zip, (Newman's word) that functioned as a punctuation mark, a period; it was a neutral bandaid color, maybe unbleached titanium, kind of whitish. On the other side of the zip, was some black painted that looked like oil dripping down, or a piece of black marble. Up close, you saw that it was just black paint that had been scraped off with a palette knife, and the canvas was showing through the scrapes. Newman was finding an economy in the way he was making the paintings that became their meaning, a key to a whole library of images. In the beginning, I'm not sure he knew that well how to do it. He was out on a limb. There was almost an abandonment about how the things were made. The succinctness and the success of his paintings was the melding of image and desire,

an object and simultaneously a picture of it, and a feeling it alluded to, I mean two opposite things that it would be possible to compress into one image.

Newman was one of the first to present the notion of a painting as a panel of meaning where different coordinates could interact. It wasn't about geometry. It wasn't about technique. The two paintings I am speaking of were made in 1949.

Mrs. Newman said that he would stay up all night worrying about one line, whether he had put it down the right way, or whether he should change it. It would drive him nuts. She showed me a little brown painting with an orange line and said that was the first painting with the zip in it. Newman put a piece of tape down so he could rehearse painting the orange line over it with his brush. He thought it was so good, that he would never be able to do it as well again so he left the piece of tape in the painting even though he originally planned to take it out. The piece of tape is still in the painting. The trace of this act makes up the history that builds the texture that is the image of his paintings, their human thread. His paintings look radically different from my own, but in my mind there is a Whitmannesque type of cataloguing used in his work as well as mine, a non-hierarchical plane where all elements of differing kind can be declared to have the same value.

Newman wasn't just making formal painting. It wasn't just stripes. I believe, if there is any, this non-hierarchical notion to be the intrinsic thread characteristic of post-war American painting. Certainly the painting that I'm interested in.

Newman's paintings have everything to do with metaphor and things that are outside of what appears to be a closed set of tools and reductivist concerns. The painting and its allusion to space are inseparable. The traces of these different acts are part of a psychodrama, a quality of invisible theater. All paintings are metaphoric. You look at it. It reminds you of something that you might have seen, a key to your imagination, not dissimilar to seeing a slogan on a wall and being able to imagine somebody painting those letters, seeing the back of his head and the stroke of his arm in the night.

'This is just to say
That I have just eaten the plums
that were in the icebox
which you where probably saving for dinner
Forgive me
They were so delicious so sweet
so cold.'
(William Carlos Williams)

To those who think painting is just about itself, I'm saying the exact opposite. The concreteness of a painting can't help but allude to a world of associations that may have a completely different face other than that of the image you are looking at. The concept of formalism imposes false limits on painting under the guise of aesthetic purity, as if such a thing could exist in real life.

21 November 1985

On the outside it may look as if art sprouts from a battle between generations. But that's not where it comes from. The art I respect, like Johns', comes from deeper inspiration than that of negating the art that was made five or ten years before. Art that is about the art world is fluff. Art that caters to critics is empty. When artists put their faith in cliques of power that they think will abet their work, they betray their class, they betray themselves. Their judgement is impaired. This destroys artists and makes them feel even more paranoid and isolated until it becomes reality. (It might become a reality no matter what you do). Artists live through and beyond their decade, even if they don't and they die. They do and their work does. Even if both get a little tattered. The mechanism of being defined as an 'artist of the sixties' or 'seventies' is a convenient marketing concept for the expendability of artists in the attempt to select and present the rare object. It also curbs and limits the possibilities of growth in the art, because it inhibits the artist from making something that's appearance is other than what was agreed upon as his work during the time of the artist's acceptance.

I want my life to be embedded in my work, crushed into my painting, like a pressed car. If it's not, my work is just some stuff. When I'm away from it, I'm crippled. Without my relationship to what may seem like these inanimate objects, I am just an indulgent misfit. If the spirit of being isn't present in the face of this work, it should be destroyed because it's meaningless. I am not making some things. I am making a synonym for the truth with all its falsehoods, oblique as it is. I am making icons that present life in terms of our death. A bouquet of mistakes.

From the Madrid notebooks, 1978

I had a funny idea that I could make a painting the size of the closet from my room in Barcelona and that I could cover it with broken plates. A rendering of the shadows of the plates on the closet seemed futile. I couldn't draw it so I thought it would be a good painting. Maybe the image of an unknown painting freed me to make a mosaic. My interest, unlike Gaudi's was not in the patterning or the design of the glazed tiles, it was in the reflective property of white plates to disturb the picture plane. The disparity between the reflectiveness of the plates and the paint meant they were in disagreement with each other and the concept of mosaic, because they fractured its homogeneity. To be honest, I didn't know what I was interested in. I was looking in wonderment at something that was all broken up. I was curious about the familiarity of the plates, their familiarity, that is, to any modern person who might be familiar with their use. I am not presupposing that Kooris that live in the bush and may not eat off plates will have the same response as people in the urban modern world, those who can remember the sound of glass breaking or plates breaking, or the sound of their parents fighting, of their parents screaming, on Krystal Nacht, as their voices are lost as they were being dragged down the streets of Berlin while pieces of shattered glass glistened in the moonlight with the apathy of little candles witnessing a child's birthday from their place on the cake; or after some great violent act, whether it be human against human or human against nature. The plates seemed to have a sound, the sound of every violent human tragedy, an anthropormorphic sense of things being smeared and thrown. I was trying to tear the mosaic out of its own body to make a bridge to something just outside of my own body. All of this was happening before I even started to paint the painting. It was that radical moment that an artist waits for. I wanted to make something that was exploding as much as I wanted to make something that was cohesive. I didn't know what the painting was supposed to look like. I didn't know how much drawing I was supposed to put on it. It was an act of desperation which I needed to hurry home to realize.

'He was mediating to engrave himself to become confused to perish'.
(Cesar Vallejo)

There's been a shift in the emphasis of art, a break with the American tradition of painting. That break will define the end of this century. It is an essential break with the basic role of the heroic.

For me art isn't about self-expression. Painting your guts out has never been an interesting idea or made an interesting painting. Feeling cannot be separated from intellect. In that sense, Neo-Expressionism doesn't exist; it never has. It's one of those terms that journalists invent for each other. The basic premise of the idea is faulty due to a lack of understanding, a deficiency reflected in their language used. 'Neo' presumes that it is a rehash of something that came before. But the political climate was different then, the concerns were different. And if expressing yourself makes an expressionist, then all artist are. But in any case what is expressed is a feeling of love for something that already existed, a response to something already felt. Cy Twombly is an expressionist; his expression is buried in the aculturated emblem of his desire, the words of dead poets scribbled in the sky; their tears are his ink.

Everything has existed before. For me there's no achievement in making a graphic description of myself, my personality, on canvas. Using used things, things we all recognize, is in direct conflict with the idea of building your own, specific original signature that will isolate the image you make from all others. Using already existing materials establishes a level of ethnographicness in the work; I mean it brings a real place and time into the aesthetic reality. Its selection can locate a place, a cultural familiar or exotic, self-made or procured. This is the platform for the mental and physical structure within the painting. The selection goes beyond the style of the signature of the artist. It is an anti-heroic art. Even if the artist is viewed as a hero and even if the involvement is viewed as heroic, the tasks and the acts are ordinary. They're only profound because they already exist.

The specialness of this art is not about some solipsistic irreducible emblem. It is about the power to take ordinary things and by arranging them to produce a kind of transcendence of their ordinariness. This transcendence is not an absolute; it doesn't preclude the possibility of things questioning themselves.

We are all stained. More and more each day these stains configure into our personalities, become our character, make us recognize and search for one another. The artist's communion with already existing materials makes it possible to commandeer prior topographical meanings for a communion of psychological ones. We are then using the physical to get at the invisible communal which is about the sameness of the viewer and the artist, not about their difference. I want to be invisible. But I want you to know I'm out there, in you. You are in me; I want to be in you. Painting makes this conversion into invisibility possible and acceptable.

11 July 1986

I saw a Van Gogh drawing of his girlfriend's mother in her back yard in Amsterdam. It was made in 1887. It has a greyish purple wash on it. There's a funny light in it. It made me feel like I was standing on Houston Street in late November, the temperature has just changed; I don't have a scarf; a friend has cancelled a dinner appointment with me.

I had nowhere to go. I felt the air go through me. I had a sense of my own twilight. That drawing made me feel like I was dead already. That's what I call Modern. Something that's appropriate, that approximates the recognition of your consciousness. That's what it means to say 'that painting looks like it was painted yesterday.' Vermeer has that power of modernness. The ability to make the viewer disappear. The quality of light gives you the sensation of sitting in any naturally lit room and witnessing the particles of air fill the room, the acuity with which it's done transcends its description of the room that's been painted and makes you sense time. It is like when you go to the movies and the lights go out and you become invisible before the film comes on. These paintings can make you recognize yourself observing observation. For a moment, you have an acute realization of your own transience, and your own explicit perception of being. This affords you the luxury of dying with a grin on your face. A sense that you actually knew what living was, then and now, even if only for a second.

We have no choice. We didn't invent this situation, but in the act of making love sometimes one can get the same satisfaction, the same clarity of beingness that makes you think it was worth all the trespasses of being here. That's what I get from those paintings. I try to make my paintings like that. That's what I want them to be about. Certainly not about the materials I use, they're just stuff, I'll use anything to make the object that will give me access to this recognition.

November 1981, Amsterdam

Julian Schnabel, 1985
Photograph by Hans Namuth

Biography and Bibliography

1951	Born in New York
1965	Moved to Brownsville, Texas
1969-73	University of Houston, Texas, BFA
1973-74	Whitney Museum Independent Study Program, New York
1975	Moved back to Texas for eight months
	Exhibition at the Contemporary Arts Museum, Houston
1976	Returned to New York; worked as a cook at Mickey Ruskin's Ocean Club Restaurant
	Travelled to Europe, visiting Paris and Milan, and lived in Tuscany until April 1977
1977	Returned to New York; worked as a cook at the Locale Restaurant until 1978
1978	Travelled to Spain, Italy and Germany and was impressed by the architecture of Antonio Gaudi in Barcelona
	First one-man show in Europe at the Galerie December, Düsseldorf

1979	First one-man show at the Mary Boone Gallery, New York (February); first 'plate' painting shown in his second show in December
1980	Met Jacqueline Beaurang in April and married her in July. Their two daughters, Lola Montes and Stella, were born in 1981 and 1983 and a son, Vito Maria, in 1986
1982	First major museum exhibition at the Stedelijk Museum, Amsterdam
1983	Began making sculpture

Lives and works in New York

Mary Boone Gallery, New York, December 1979

One Man Exhibitions

1976   Contemporary Art Museum, Houston
1978   Galerie December, Düsseldorf
1979   Mary Boone Gallery, New York
           Daniel Weinberg Gallery, San Francisco
           Mary Boone Gallery, New York
1980   Galerie Bruno Bischofberger, Zürich
           Young/Hoffman Gallery, Chicago
1981   Mary Boone/Leo Castelli Gallery, New York
1982   Stedelijk Museum, Amsterdam
           Galerie Bruno Bischofberger, Zürich
           Margo Leavin Gallery, Los Angeles
           Museum of Contemporary Art, Los Angeles
           Daniel Weinberg Gallery, San Francisco
           University Art Museum, Berkeley
           Tate Gallery, London
           Mary Boone Gallery, New York
1983   Galerie Bruno Bischofberger, Zürich
           Castelli Graphics, New York
           Leo Castelli Gallery, New York
           Akron Art Museum, Akron, Ohio
           Galerie Daniel Templon, Paris
           Galleria Mario Diacono, Rome
           Waddington Galleries, London
           Akira Ikeda Gallery, Nagoya, Japan
1984   Akira Ikeda Gallery, Tokyo
           Galerie Bruno Bischofberger, Zürich
           The Pace Gallery, New York
1985   Galerie Bruno Bischofberger, Zürich
           Galleria Gian Enzo Sperone, Rome
           Waddington Galleries, London

Selected Group Exhibitions

1971   *Hidden Houston*, University of St. Thomas, Houston
1972   Louisiana Gallery, Houston
1974   *W.I.S.P. Exhibition*, Whitney Museum of American Art, New York
1977   *Surrogate/Self Portraits*, Holly Solomon Gallery, New York
1979   *Visionary Images*, Renaissance Society, University of Chicago, Chicago
           Four Artists, Hallwalls, Buffalo, New York
1980   *Nuova Imagine*, Milan
           L'Amérique aux Indépendants, Grand Palais, Paris
           La Biennale di Venezia, Venice
           Drawings, Mary Boone Gallery, New York
1981   *A New Spirit in Painting*, Royal Academy of Arts, London
           Biennial Exhibition, Whitney Museum of American Art, New York
           Westkunst: Heute, Cologne
           Schnabel, Rothenberg, Moskovitz, Kunsthalle, Basel; travelled to Kunstverein, Frankfurt and Louisiana Museum, Humlebaek, Denmark
           The Contemporary Image, Akron Art Institute, Akron, Ohio
1982   *Issues: New Allegory*, Institute of Contemporary Art, Boston
           60/80: Attitudes, Concepts, Images, Stedelijk Museum, Amsterdam
           74th American Exhibition, Art Institute of Chicago, Chicago
           La Biennale di Venezia, Venice
           Trans-Avanguardia, Galleria Civica, Modena
           New Paintings by Chia, Clemente, Kiefer, Salle and Schnabel, Anthony d'Offay Gallery, London
           The Americans: Collage 1950-82, Contemporary Arts

Stedelijk Museum, Amsterdam 1982

Museum, Houston
Zeitgeist, Martin-Gropius-Bau, Berlin
The Expressionist Image, Sidney Janis Gallery,
New York
New York Now, Kestner-Gesellschaft, Hannover

1983 *Biennial Exhibition*, Whitney Museum of American
Art, New York
The New Art, Tate Gallery, London
The First Show, Museum of Contemporary Art,
Los Angeles
Tendencias en Nueva York, Palacio de Velasquez,
Madrid; travelled to Fundaçio Joan Miró, Barcelona
and Musée du Luxembourg, Paris

1984 *An International Survey of Recent Painting and
Sculpture*, Museum of Modern Art, New York
The Heroic Figure, Contemporary Arts Museum,
Houston
Terrae Motus, Istituto per l'Arte Contemporanea,
Naples
Rosc '84, Dublin
Legendes, Musée d'Art Contemporain, Bordeaux
The Meditative Surface, Renaissance Society,
University of Chicago, Chicago
La Grande Parade, Stedelijk Museum, Amsterdam

1985 *Nouvelle Biennale de Paris*, Paris
Carnegie International, Museum of Art, Carnegie
Institute, Pittsburgh

Mary Boone Gallery, New York 1982

Leo Castelli Gallery, New York 1983

Selected Bibliography

1975 DeAk, Edit, 'Julian Schnabel', *Art-Rite Magazine*, May
1975

1978 'Julian Schnabel', *Domus*, January 1978

1979 Zimmer, William, 'Julian Schnabel: New Painting', *Soho
Weekly News*, 22-28 February 1979, p. 31
Anderson, Ali, 'Voice Choices: Julian Schnabel',
The Village Voice, 26 February 1979, p. 31
Bleckner, Ross, 'Transcendent Anti-Fetishism',
Artforum, March 1979 p. 50
Tatransky, Valentin, 'Julian Schnabel', *Artforum*, May
1979, p. 36
Rickey, Carrie, 'Julian Schnabel', *Artforum*, May 1979,
p. 59
Ratcliff, Carter, 'Visionary Images: Emblematic
Figuration', catalogue essay for *Visionary Images*,
Renaissance Society, University of Chicago, 1979
Rickey, Carrie, 'What Becomes a Legend Most?',
The Village Voice, 22 October 1979, p. 91
Ricard, René, 'Julian Schnabel's Plate Painting at Mary
Boone', *Art in America*, November 1979, p. 86
Tatransky, Valentin, 'Four Artists', *Arts Magazine*,
December 1979, p. 25

1980 Politi, Giancarlo, 'An Interview with Harald Szeemann',
Flash Art, Summer 1980, pp. 5-7
Zimmer, William, 'Artbreakers: New York's Emerging
Artists', *Soho News* 17-23 September 1980, pp. 33-48
Ratcliff, Carter, 'Art to Art: Julian Schnabel',
Interview Magazine, October 1980, pp. 55-57
Kertess, Klaus, 'Figuring it out', *Artforum*, November
1980, pp. 30-35

1981 Feaver, William, 'UK 8, Germany 11', *The Observer
Review*, January 1981, p. 28

Hughes, Robert, 'Quirks, Clamors and Variety', *Time Magazine*, 2 March 1981

Morgan, Stuart, 'A New Spirit in Painting', *Artforum*, April 1981, p. 47

Smith, Roberta, 'Biennial Blues', *Art in America*, April 1981, p. 92-101

Levin, Kim, 'Art: Julian Schnabel', *The Village Voice*, 15-21 April 1981

Kramer, Hilton, 'Art: Two Painters Explore New Wave', *The New York Times*, 17 April 1981, p. 17

Perrault, John, 'Is Julian Schnabel That Good?', *The Soho News*, 22 April 1981, p. 63

Schjeldahl, Peter, 'Bravery in Action', *The Village Voice*, 29 April 1981, p. 81

Stevens, Mark, 'Bull in the China Shop', *Newsweek*, 11 May 1981, p. 79

Feaver, William, 'A New Spirit - or Just a Tired Ghost?', *Artnews*, May 1981, pp. 114-118

Kramer, Hilton, 'Expressionism Returns to Painting', *The New York Times*, 12 July 1981, Section 2, p. 1

Ricard, René, 'Not About Julian Schnabel', *Artforum*, Summer 1981 pp. 74-80

Smith, Roberta, 'Fresh Paint?', *Art in America*, Summer 1981, pp. 70-79

Lawson, Thomas, 'Last Exit: Painting', *Artforum*, October 1981, pp. 40-47

Oliva, Achille Bonito, 'The International Trans-Avantgarde', *Flash Art*, October-November 1981, pp. 36-43

Kuspit, Donald, 'The New Expressionism: Art as

The Pace Gallery, New York 1984

Damaged Goods', *Artforum*, November 1981, pp. 47-55

Hager, Steven, 'The Schnabel Effect', *Horizon Magazine*, December 1981, pp. 42-49

1982 Ricard, René, 'About Julian Schnabel', catalogue, Stedelijk Museum, Amsterdam, January 1982

van Grevenstein, Alexander, 'Julian Schnabel, The American Sublime', catalogue, Stedelijk Museum, Amsterdam, January 1982

Pincus-Witten, Robert, 'Julian Schnabel: Blind Faith', *Arts Magazine* February 1982, pp. 152-155

Haden-Guest, Anthony, 'The New Queen of the Art Scene', *New York Magazine*, 19 April 1982, pp. 24-30

Groot, Paul, 'The Spirit of Documenta', *Flash Art*, Summer 1982, pp. 20-25

Ratcliff, Carter, 'Contemporary American Art', *Flash Art*, Summer 1982, pp. 32-35

Francis, Richard, 'Julian Schnabel', catalogue, Tate Gallery, June 1982

Januszczak, Waldemar, 'Nothing succeeds like excess', *The Guardian*, 30 June 1982

Packer, William, 'Expressionism is back in fashion', *Financial Times*, 6 July 1982

Taylor, John Russell, 'Integrity against fashion', *The Times*, 6 July 1982

Vaizey, Marina, 'How to become an old master', *The Sunday Times*, 7 July 1982

Cork, Richard, 'Storm on a tea-cup', *Evening Standard*, 8 July 1982

Feaver, William, 'A bad case of hype', *The Observer*, 11 July 1982

Leo Castelli Gallery, New York 1983

Gooding, Mel, 'Julian Schnabel', *Arts Review*,
16 July 1982

Morgan, Stuart, 'Misunderstanding Schnabel', *Artscribe*,
August 1982, No. 36, pp. 44-49

Collings, Matthew, 'Julian Schnabel at the Tate Gallery',
Artscribe, August 1982, No. 36, p. 56

Fuller, Peter, 'Plus ça change...', *Art Monthly*,
September 1982

Walker, John A., 'Julian Schnabel at the Tate', *Aspects*,
Autumn 1982, No. 20

Geelhaar, Christian, 'Julian Schnabel's Head (for
Albert)', *Arts Magazine*, October 1982. pp. 74-75

Hughes, Robert, 'Expressionist Bric-a-Brac', *Time*,
1 November 1982, p. 71

Kramer, Hilton, 'The New Expressionism: Signs of
Passion', *The New Criterion*, November 1982, pp. 40-45

1983   Robbins, David, 'Julian Schnabel', catalogue,
Waddington Galleries, November 1983

'Julian Schnabel', *Current Biography*, November 1983,
Vol. 44, No. 11

McEwen, John, 'The golden age of junk art',
The Sunday Times, 18 December 1983

Kramer, Hilton, 'Julian Schnabel', *Art of Our Time*,
The Saatchi Collection, Lund Humphries, London
1984, pp. 25-28

1984   Fuller, Peter, 'Julian Schnabel', *Art Monthly*, February
1984

Hill, Andrea, 'Julian Schnabel at Waddington', *Artscribe*,
February-April 1984, No. 45, pp. 58-60

Zacharopoulos, Denys, 'Julian Schnabel, Galerie
Daniel Templon, *Artforum*, April 1984, pp. 90-91

Morgan, Stuart, 'Drift', catalogue, *The Fifth Biennale
of Sydney, Private Symbol: Social Metaphor*, April 1984

Kuspit, Donald, 'Julian Schnabel's Profundity: Not an
Apologia Pro Vita Sua', *C Magazine*, Autumn 1984,
pp. 16-19

Schiff, Gert, 'Julian Schnabel', catalogue,
The Pace Gallery, New York, November 1984

Brenson, M., 'Art: Julian Schnabel The Carnival Man',
New York Times, 9 November 1984

Danto, Arthur, 'Julian Schnabel', *The Nation*,
8 December 1984, pp. 624-626

1985   Kuspit, Donald, 'The Rhetoric of Rawness: Its Effects
on Meaning in Julian Schnabel's Paintings', *Arts
Magazine*, March 1985, pp. 126-130

Marzorati, G., 'Julian Schnabel: Plate It as It Lays',
ARTnews, April 1985

Kuspit, Donald, 'Julian Schnabel', catalogue,
Waddington Galleries, October 1985

Januszczak, Waldemar, 'Schnabel', *The Guardian*,
8 October 1985

Morgan, Stuart, 'Letters to a Wound', *Artscribe*,
International December/January 1985/86, No. 55,
pp. 32-37

Statements and Writings by the Artist

1982   Untitled statement in *Julian Schnabel* Tate Gallery
catalogue

'For Willem de Kooning', *Willem de Kooning:
The North Atlantic Light 1960-83*, Stedelijk Museum,
Amsterdam, 1983

1984   'The Patients and the Doctors', *Artforum*, February
1984, pp. 54-59

Interviews

1982   'Expressionism Today: An Artists' Symposium',
interview with Hayden Herrera, *Art in America*,
December 1982, pp. 58-75, 139, 141

1983   'Julian Schnabel interviewed by Stuart Morgan',
Artscribe, December 1983, No. 44, pp. 15-21

1986   'Modern Art', Julian Schnabel interviewed by Matthew
Collings, *Artscribe International*, September 1986,
No. 59, pp. 26-31

The Pace Gallery, New York 1984

The Whitechapel Art Gallery opened in 1901 and is administered by a charitable trust. The trust has no endowment and the Gallery's existence and programme therefore depend wholly on financial assistance given by national and local authorities, companies (through sponsorship and donations), foundations, trusts and individuals.

The Whitechapel gratefully acknowledges the financial assistance which it has been receiving from:

Arts Council of Great Britain   Greater London Arts
London Borough of Tower Hamlets
Inner London Education Authority

Foundations and Trusts
Aldgate and Allhallows Barking Exhibition Foundation
Clothworkers' Company   Drapers' Company
Grocers' Company   The Henry Moore Foundation
Mercers' Company   Merchant Taylors' Company
Ruskin's Guild of St. George Sir John Cass's Foundation

Sponsors
British Petroleum Company plc

Corporate Patrons
Cable and Wireless plc   Citicorp Investment Bank
City Acre Property Investment Trust
E D & F Man International Ltd   English Trust Company Ltd
Euromoney   Granada Group plc
Hogg Robinson (Travel) Ltd   Midland Bank plc
The Morgan Bank   Morgan Stanley International
National Westminster Bank plc   Philip Morris Ltd
Saatchi & Saatchi Compton plc
Salomon Brothers International Ltd   Sedgwick Group plc
Waddington Galleries Ltd   Watney, Mann and Truman Ltd
William Lea & Co Ltd

Corporate Associates
Anthony d'Offay Gallery   The Bank of England
BET plc   Christie, Manson & Woods Ltd
The Fine Art Society   Juda Rowan Gallery
Kleinwort, Benson, Lonsdale plc
Lisson Gallery London Ltd
Marlborough Fine Art (London) Ltd   Mayor Gallery Ltd
Morgan Grenfell & Co Ltd   MoMart Ltd
Robert Fleming Holdings Ltd   N M Rothschild & Sons Ltd
Sun Life Assurance Society plc
Victoria Miro Gallery London   S G Warburg Ltd

Catalogue published by the Trustees of the Whitechapel Art Gallery, London
© The Authors and the Trustees of the Whitechapel Art Gallery, 1986
Edited by Nicholas Serota and Joanna Skipwith
Designed by Richard Smith at Peter Saville Associates, London
Printed in Holland by Lecturis bv, Eindhoven
3000 copies printed and paperbound, September 1986
ISBN 0 85488 070 4